Get INVOLVED

Emma Heyderman   Patricia Reilly

Get INVOLVED!

Collaborative projects

Collaborate with your classmates to develop your problem-solving skills in the WDYT? projects. Become an expert on a topic and get involved with others in your class.

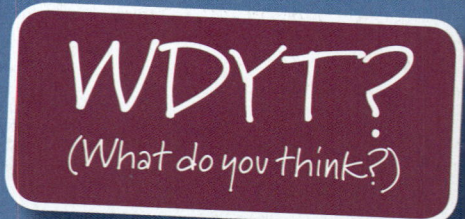

Real-world content

Learn about culture while you learn English. *Get Involved!* is full of real-world content, so go online and learn more about the people, events and places in the book.

Super skills

Get Involved! helps develop your critical thinking, collaboration, creativity and communication skills, which are essential for life in the 21st century.

COLLABORATION **CRITICAL THINKING**

COMMUNICATION **CREATIVITY**

Building skills for the real world

Social and emotional learning

Get Involved! helps you develop strategies to deal with social situations and gives you the vocabulary you need to discuss emotions that you or others experience.

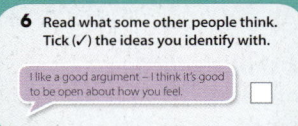

Media-rich content

Get Involved! videos help you with critical thinking, communication and project presentations and improve your video literacy skills.
Access On-the-Go Practice on your phone through the Macmillan Student's App and improve your English with gamified content.

Inclusive classroom

Show your strengths and talents by putting your investigative skills and logic to the test with *Get Involved!* Brain teasers. Learn at your own pace with graded Workbook activities and The longer read.

1 ☆ Complete the sentences with the words in the box.

2 ☆☆ Read the essay titles. Match the sentences in exercise 1 with each title.

3

UNIT	VOCABULARY	GRAMMAR	READING AND CRITICAL THINKING
STARTER What do you know? Page 6	**Vocabulary:** entertainment, house and home, adjective order, sports		
1 All about me WDYT? What makes you the person you are? Page 12	Personal qualities Describing personal characteristics Phrasal verbs: three-part verbs 🎥 Personality types	Past tenses Present perfect simple and present perfect continuous Past perfect simple and past simple Past perfect simple and past perfect continuous	A magazine article *This is me!* **Subskill:** Keeping a record of vocabulary
2 Welcome to the future! WDYT? What changes would you like to see in the future? Page 24	Describing products Changes Expressions with *get* 🎥 Predicting technology	Future tenses Future continuous and future perfect Future time expressions	A scientific report *Innovations that will rock our world* **Subskill:** Predicting content
3 Perfect WDYT? What's your perfect day? Page 36	Social media Influencers Word formation: nouns 🎥 How to create great content	Relative clauses Comparing	An article *Fifteen minutes of fame!* **Subskill:** Understanding the writer's purpose
4 Natural world WDYT? What is the best way to enjoy nature? Page 48	Places Natural world Words that are nouns and verbs 🎥 Exploring the island of East Java	Modal verbs Perfect modals	A travel guide *The Seven Wonders* **Subskill:** Identifying fact and opinion
5 Communicate WDYT? What makes a good communicator? Page 60	Reporting verbs Ways of talking Word formation: prefixes 🎥 Perfect presentations	Reported speech: statements Reported speech: questions Reported speech: orders and requests Reporting verbs	A history essay *A brief history of sharing news* **Subskill:** Understanding formal language
6 Challenges WDYT? What can you do to challenge yourself? Page 72	People Challenges Television 🎥 Things I've learnt about failure	Conditionals Alternatives to *if* *I wish* and *If only* *I wish* + *would/wouldn't*	An opinion article *The BIG question: Do you need a rival to be successful?* **Subskill:** Finding evidence in the text
7 Going unplugged WDYT? Could you unplug for a day, a week, a month or even longer? Page 84	Lifestyle Chilling out, getting active Expressions with *make* and *do* 🎥 A week without social media	The passive The passive: modal verbs *have/get something done*	An article *Are you ready to unplug?* **Subskill:** Referencing
8 Make a difference WDYT? How can you contribute to make society better? Page 96	Global issues Phrasal verbs for achieving goals 🎥 Plogging	Verb patterns *used to, be used to, get used to*	An article *Emoji for all* **Subskill:** Summarising a text in your own words
9 Look what you know! Page 108	**Vocabulary** and **Grammar** review		**Reading:** review of subskills
	Pronunciation p116	Project planner p118	

LISTENING	REAL-WORLD SPEAKING	WRITING	PRONUNCIATION	PROJECT
Grammar: present simple and present continuous, past simple and present perfect, past simple and past continuous, *some-/any-/no-/every-* compounds, future tense review				
Short interviews about personality quizzes **Subskill:** Dealing with homophones	Solving shopping issues	A description of a person **Subskill:** Gradable and non-gradable adjectives + adverbs	/h/ Homophones	Create a poster about your personal identity including a self-portrait and a description of yourself. **Communication** Using visuals to communicate your ideas
An informal conversation between two friends on pros and cons of robots **Subskill:** Understanding the speaker's attitude	Organising an event	A product review **Subskill:** Connectors of contrast	/æ/, /ɑː/ and /eɪ/ Intonation	Imagine you have travelled to the future. Give a presentation to the class on the changes you see. **Creativity** Getting inspiration from others
A radio interview about happiness **Subskill:** Listening for the information you need	Telling an anecdote	An opinion essay **Subskill:** Organising your essay	/b/ and /v/ /ʃ/ and /tʃ/	Create a 'What's your perfect day?' video for a class YouTube channel. **Collaboration** Successfully completing the task as a team
A podcast about why we love natural disaster films **Subskill:** Using prior knowledge	Giving instructions	A description of a place **Subskill:** Using articles correctly	Word stress: nouns and verbs	Create a proposal for a place in your country or abroad to be made a Natural Wonder of the World. Film your group presenting your proposal. **Critical thinking** Synthesising information
A podcast about misunderstandings **Subskill:** Understanding rapid speech	Discussing opinions	A report **Subskill:** Presenting key findings	Connected speech: word linking	Give a persuasive presentation on why you should be given a travel scholarship. **Communication** Giving a persuasive presentation
A radio phone-in programme about TV talent shows **Subskill:** Inferring meaning	Checking understanding and clarifying	An informal article **Subskill:** Writing for an audience	Sentence stress in conditionals	Give a presentation about a TV talent show that you have invented. **Creativity** Developing and implementing new ideas
An informal conversation about how to get around without a mobile **Subskill:** Understanding words from context	Giving directions	A for-and-against essay **Subskill:** Using connectors of reason	Word stress: expressions with *make* and *do*	Plan an Unplugging Day for your school and present your leaflet proposal to your class. **Critical thinking** Building a powerful argument
A radio interview about Lual Mayen **Subskill:** Correcting mistakes	Politely interrupting	A formal letter of complaint **Subskill:** Using formal language	Intonation when interrupting	Design a new emoji and create a digital poster to justify the need for it. **Collaboration** Respecting others
Listening: review of subskills		**Speaking:** review of Key phrases		**Writing:** review of subskills

Phrasebook p122   Irregular verbs p126

STARTER — What do you know?

What's on?
Vocabulary: entertainment

1 🔊 1 Read and listen to the article. Match headings a–c with paragraphs 1–3.
- **a** Start watching a TV series
- **b** Read more
- **c** Enjoy music outside

KEEPING A PROMISE TO YOURSELF

How often do you make a promise to yourself (or others) at the start of a school year, only to break it? Follow our suggestions below to help you keep your promises.

1 (…)
If you find most **bestsellers** hard work and you actually prefer pictures to words, why not start with a **graphic novel**? Manga Shakespeare has **released** a series of books which combine a simple version of Shakespeare's plays with manga illustrations.

2 (…)
Are you getting bored of school concerts or **gigs** in dark **venues**? How about going to an outdoor music festival? Larmer Tree Festival is a festival for all ages where you can see your favourite **artists** on stage, enjoy street theatre and learn new skills at a range of workshops.

3 (…)
We suggest you try *Sherlock*. With its exceptional **cast**, you'll be hooked from the first **episode**. It was first **broadcast** in 2010 and every **season** is entertaining. *Sherlock* is **set** in 21st century London and appeals to **audiences** all over the world.

2 Copy and complete the diagram with the words in bold in the article in exercise 1. Then add the words in the box.

> chapter   critic   plot   review   script

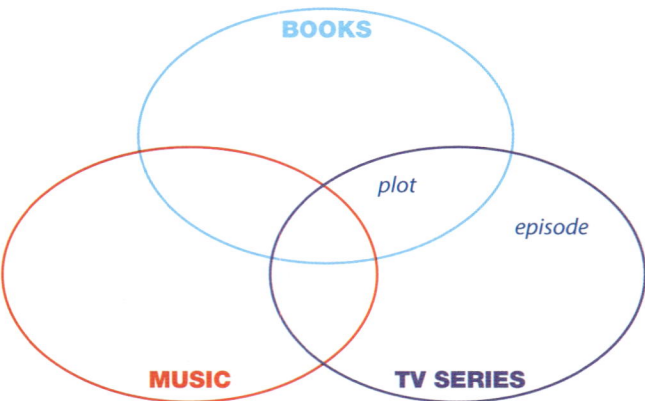

BOOKS — *plot* — *episode* — MUSIC — TV SERIES

3 What is the difference in meaning between each pair of words?
1. a chapter/an episode
2. a critic/a review
3. a bestseller/a graphic novel
4. a venue/a gig
5. a plot/a script

Grammar: present simple and present continuous

4 Read the examples and complete the rules with *present simple* or *present continuous*.

> How often **do** you **make** a promise to yourself?
> This series **combines** a simple version of a story with manga illustrations.
> I **promise** to read more this year.
> I'**m reading** a great bestseller at the moment.
> **Are** you **getting** bored of gigs in small venues?

We use the **1** (…) for actions in progress or a developing situation.

We use the **2** (…) for facts, habits and routines.

We don't use the **3** (…) with state verbs like *believe*, *promise* and *understand*.

Starter

5 Complete the text with the present simple or present continuous form of the verbs in brackets.

 Log in

Q What **1** (…) you (…) **(read)** right now?

 We **2** (…) **(have)** to read *Lord of the Flies* for school, so I **3** (…) **(read)** that at the moment. I **4** (…) **(enjoy)** it so far. It **5** (…) **(be)** about a group of boys who end up alone on a desert island. I **6** (…) **(not want)** to spoil the ending for you, but this book **7** (…) **(say)** a lot about human nature.
Ned Jones

 We **8** (…) **(need)** to read *The Curious Incident of the Dog in the Night-Time* for school, so I **9** (…) **(not read)** anything else. It **10** (…) **(tell)** the story of a boy with autism who **11** (…) **(want)** to solve the murder of a dog. It **12** (…) **(not be)** a typical book, though. It **13** (…) **(begin)** with Chapter 2 and the chapter numbers **14** (…) **(not follow)** a logical order.
Ester Cuesta

6 Read the information and look at the pairs of sentences. What is the difference in meaning between a and b?

> **Verb meaning in present simple and present continuous**
>
> Some verbs have a different meaning in the present simple and present continuous. For example:
> *This book **smells** of an old book shop.* (It has a particular smell.)
> *Why **are** you **smelling** that book?* (Put your nose close to something to sniff it.)

1 a My friend's dad **has** a pizza restaurant in town.
  b We**'re having** dinner there right now.
2 a I **think** Billie Eilish is an amazing singer.
  b I**'m thinking** of getting a ticket for her concert.
3 a My cousin**'s** usually a little unfriendly.
  b He **isn't being** unfriendly today because he's in a good mood.
4 a That **looks** really difficult. Is it?
  b I**'m looking** at instructions right now.
5 a I **see** what you mean!
  b I**'m seeing** the hockey coach at break today.

Grammar: past simple and present perfect

7 Read the examples and choose the correct option to complete the rules.

> The BBC first released *Sherlock* in 2010.
> Benedict Cumberbatch has played Sherlock Holmes ever since then.

1 We use the **past simple/present perfect** to talk about completed actions in the past with expressions which specify the time they happened.
2 We use the **past simple/present perfect** to talk about actions in the past without specifying when they happened.

8 Copy and complete the table with the time expressions in the box. What is the difference between *for* and *since*?

> ever/never   ~~for six months~~   in July   last week
> lately   recently   since 2019   three years ago
> ~~when I was younger~~   yesterday

Past simple	Present perfect
when I was younger	for six months

9 Complete the dialogue with the correct past simple or present perfect form of the verbs in brackets.

Natalie: **1** (…) you (…) **(see)** anything good lately?
Chris: Yeah! We **2** (…) **(go)** to the theatre to see *Hamilton* on Saturday.
Natalie: Cool! I **3** (…) **(not see)** that musical. What **4** (…) **(be)** it like?
Chris: I **5** (…) **(think)** it **6** (…) **(be)** amazing. What about you? **7** (…) you (…) **(go)** to see anything recently?
Natalie: I **8** (…) **(not do)** anything very exciting since we last **9** (…) **(speak)**, but yesterday I **10** (…) **(finish)** the book you **11** (…) **(give)** me for my birthday.
Chris: What **12** (…) you (…) **(think)** of it?
Natalie: I **13** (…) **(love)** it. What an original plot!

10 💬 Work in pairs. Ask and answer the questions.

1 Do you prefer to watch films at home or at the cinema? Why?
2 Which TV series are you watching at the moment?
3 Have you read a good book lately? What was it about?

7

 **Starter**

My house
Vocabulary: house and home

1 🔊 2 Read and listen to the text. Do British prime ministers still live in this house?

OPEN HOUSE

If you could look inside someone's house, whose would you choose? Once a year, for a weekend, many cities around the world open up iconic houses and buildings to everyone for free. Here's one of our favourites:

10 DOWNING STREET, LONDON, UK

The British prime minister's London **terraced** house is easily recognisable with its hanging **lamp** outside and shiny black **front door** with a lion-shaped **doorknocker**. Before you go inside, take another look at the door. The **doorbell** doesn't actually work and forget about using a key – there isn't a **keyhole** anywhere! Don't worry though, there's always somebody waiting inside in the **entrance hall** to let visitors in.

The **ground floor** rooms are mainly used for government business and entertaining, and the kitchen is in the **basement**. All the way up the impressive **staircase** and along each **landing**, you'll find black and white **portraits** of past prime ministers hung in order. The prime minister used to have a private **flat** on the **top floor**, but in recent times, they have used the bigger flat next door in Number 11.

2 Check the meaning of the words in bold in the text in exercise 1. Copy and complete the table. Add the words in the box.

| attic/loft   corridor   cottage   detached |
| fireplace   semi-detached |

Type of house	Place in the house	Features of a house
terraced	entrance hall	lamp

3 🔊 3 Listen to Andrea talking to Rob. Answer the questions.
1 Whose house did Rob visit?
2 What did he think of it?
3 What was his favourite room? Why?

Grammar: past simple and past continuous

4 Read the examples and answer the questions.

> He **recorded** tracks for his last two albums there.
> While we **were visiting** my cousins in Memphis, we **went** to Graceland Mansion.

1 Which tense do we use for completed actions in the past?
2 Which tense do we use for an activity in progress in the past?
3 How do we form the negative and question of each tense?

5 Correct one mistake in each sentence.
1 My dad didn't lived here when he was younger.
2 While I was cleaning the basement, I come across an old clock.
3 Was you having dinner when I called?
4 She couldn't hear you because she was listen to loud music.
5 Did you went out for lunch at the weekend?

6 Complete the sentences with the correct past simple or past continuous form of the verbs in the box.

| appear   break   clean out   come down   fall |
| find   hurt   leave   not play   not recognise   ring |

1 We (…) the attic when we (…) an old box of photos.
2 Someone (…) their keys in the keyhole, so I (…) the doorbell.
3 While my sister (…) the stairs with the suitcase, she (…) and (…) herself.
4 My friends (…) football when the window (…).
5 I (…) your brother when he (…) on the landing.

7 💬 Work in pairs. Complete the questions with your own ideas in the past simple or past continuous. Ask and answer the questions.
1 Where did you live when (…)?
2 When you were at primary school, did (…)?
3 What (…) at 7:30 pm yesterday evening?
4 When the teacher started the class, were (…)?

Starter

Grammar: some-/any-/no-/every- compounds

8 Read the examples and choose the correct option to complete the rules.

> Many cities around the world open up iconic houses and buildings to everyone for free.
> No-one has a key for 10 Downing Street.
> Don't worry, there's always somebody waiting inside.
> There isn't anybody living on the ground floor.

1. *-body* and *-one* have **the same/a different** meaning.
2. We generally use **some-/any-** compounds in positive sentences and **some-/any-** compounds in negative sentences.
3. In most questions, we use **some-/any-** compounds, but for offers, we use **some-/any-** compounds.
4. We don't use *no* or *not* with **no-/any-** compounds.

9 Complete the sentences with the correct *some-/any-/no-* or *every-* compound.

1. I need (…) colourful for my room. It's looking a bit plain.
2. She's looked (…) for her old white trainers, but she can't find them (…) .
3. My aunt was walking (…) near the coast when she found this wonderful shell.
4. I don't need (…) else for my room. I like empty shelves.
5. Please don't tell (…) about the party. It's a surprise.
6. When the teacher asked the class, there was silence. (…) knew the answer.

10 Work in pairs. Ask and answer the questions.

1. Does everyone in your class live in a flat?
2. Has anybody in your family ever played a gig?
3. If you could live anywhere in the world, where would you live?
4. At the end of a busy week, do you prefer doing nothing or doing something active?

Vocabulary: adjective order

11 Read the tip box at the bottom of the page. Then complete the sentences with the adjectives in the correct order.

1. There used to be a(n) (…) portrait above the fireplace. **(beautiful / old / big)**
2. I got this (…) bag for my birthday. **(brown / leather / small)**
3. I was looking for some trainers when I bought these (…) boots. **(black / rubber / trendy)**
4. My sister's just bought some (…) glasses. **(Italian / metal / round)**
5. My cousins have lived in a(n) (…) loft since they moved to New York. **(amazing / brand new / large)**
6. I saw an advertisement online for a (…) racing bike. **(aluminium / cool / second-hand)**

12 Write a description of your dream room. What is it like? Why do you like it so much?

Adjective order							
When two or more adjectives come before a noun, they usually follow this order.							
	Opinion	Size	Age	Shape	Colour	Origin	Material	Noun
a	beautiful	large	old	square	red	Italian	plastic	box
Remember, we rarely use more than two or three adjectives before a noun and we never use adjectives in the plural: we say *plastic boxes* and not ~~*plastics boxes*~~.							

Starter

Take it up!

Vocabulary: sports

1 Which of these sports are used with *do*, *go* and *play*? Have you tried any of them?

> athletics   climbing   cycling
> gymnastics   hockey   skateboarding
> tennis   volleyball   yoga

I sometimes go skateboarding, but I've never done yoga or been climbing.

2 What are the differences in meaning between each set of words?
   1 **hold**, **break** and **set** a record
   2 **train**, **practise** and **compete**
   3 **lose**, **beat**, **draw** and **win**
   4 a **game**, a **match** and a **tournament**
   5 an **athlete**, a **coach** and a **referee**

3 Read the text about breaking. What do the words in bold have in common?

Breaking, which originally **comes from** New York City, is a competitive dance form. B-girls and B-boys **compete in** 'dance battles' which **consist of** high-energy steps **set to** hip hop music. A panel of judges **award** points **for** things like creativity, personality and technique. Some people say 'break' **refers to** how the DJ **changes from** one track **to** another. So why does the International Olympic Committee plan to **include** it **in** the Olympics? They hope to **connect with** more young athletes by **moving** sports **out of** stadiums and **into** the city.

Collocations

When you make a note of a new vocabulary item, make sure you write down and learn any words that go with it, e.g. (play) football, (do) breaking, (do) yoga, compete (in), consist (of), etc.

Grammar: future tense review

4 Read the examples and look at the verbs in bold. What are some of the different forms we can use to talk about the future?
   a We**'re competing** in a tennis tournament in June.
   b Rita's beating him 7–0 – she**'s going to win**!
   c I'm bored. I know, I**'ll ring** Kevin to see if he fancies going skateboarding.
   d The match **starts** at 10:00 am tomorrow – don't be late!
   e I think sport **will be** very different in the future.
   f My team**'s going to train** at the sports stadium this season.

5 Look at the examples in exercise 4 again. Match uses 1–6 with examples a–f.
   1 a decision made at the moment
   2 a future arrangement with a fixed date
   3 a prediction with little evidence now
   4 a timetabled event
   5 a prediction with evidence now
   6 a plan or decision made before

6 Complete the sentences with the words and phrases in the box.

> 'm changing   'm going to take up
> 's going to rain   starts   will beat

   1 Training (…) next week.
   2 I (…) from tennis to volleyball from Monday.
   3 I (…) yoga this term.
   4 I think our team (…) an important rival later this month.
   5 It (…) all afternoon – look at those clouds!

7 Write a question for each of the sentences in exercise 6.
   1 *When does training start?*

8 💬 Work in pairs. Ask and answer the questions in exercise 7.

> When does training start?
>
>> Hockey training starts next week, but swimming doesn't start until the end of September.

Starter

What's in this book?

1 Look through your book. Who, what or where are these?

2 Look more closely at Unit 1. Match features 1–8 with a–h.

1 WDYT?
2 VIDEO SKILLS
3 CRITICAL THINKING
4 BRAIN TEASER
5 GRAMMAR ROUND-UP
6 Research
7 QUICK REVIEW
8 FINAL REFLECTION

a a fun grammar exercise
b an exercise where you reflect on the process of doing the project
c an exercise where you practise all the grammar you've learnt so far
d a question that comes at the beginning of every unit, to get you thinking about the topic
e an exercise that helps you to explore the ideas in the reading text more deeply
f a section of the unit that summarises all the new grammar and vocabulary
g an activity where you have to find out more about something online
h a section where you watch and think about different kinds of video clips

3 Now explore the rest of the book and answer the questions. Can you answer them all in two minutes?

1 How many units are there in the book?
2 How many pages are there in each main unit?
3 What do you always learn first in each unit?
4 Where can you check irregular verbs?
5 How many pages of Phrasebook are there at the end of the book?
6 What can you find on pp4–5?
7 In which unit will you review everything you have learnt?
8 What can you find on pp118–121?

THE CLASSROOM CHALLENGE

4 Match topics A–H with Units 1–8 in this book. Can you be the first to finish?

A the key to happiness
B some misunderstandings
C personality quizzes
D the UN Sustainable Development Goals
E a review of a technological device
F finding your way without a phone
G do you need a rival to be successful?
H nominating a Natural Wonder of the World

1 All about me

(What do you think?)

Vocabulary: personal qualities; describing personal characteristics; phrasal verbs: three-part verbs

Grammar: past tenses; present perfect simple and continuous; past perfect simple and past simple; past perfect simple and continuous

Reading: a magazine article about clothes and identity

Listening: short interviews about personality quizzes

Speaking: solving shopping issues

Writing: a description of a person

Project: create a poster about personal identity

Video skills p13

Real-world speaking p19

Project pp22–23

What makes you the person you are?

Personal qualities

1 Look at the adjectives in the box. Can you add any more personality adjectives?

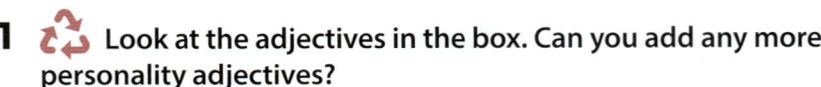

confident   creative   enthusiastic   generous   hard-working
patient   polite   reliable   sensible   sociable

2 Work in pairs. Use the adjectives in exercise 1 to describe your friends and family.

I think my mum is generous and sociable.

My best friend is confident and hard-working.

3 Which adjectives form an opposite with negative prefixes *un-* or *im-*?

reliable – unreliable

SHAPE AND IDENTITY

Vocabulary

When we look at characters from video games and comics, their shape can tell us a lot about their identity.

1 This shape is solid, like a mountain, and shows many characteristics. Characters with this shape are often strong and confident, but they can also be big and scary or kind and **clumsy**. They're often **determined** like typical superheroes. They can be a little **stubborn**.

2 This is the most dynamic shape and it is often used to show danger and villains. Sharp lines and angles can make characters appear **aggressive** or **arrogant** and **selfish**, and suggest they might be **cruel**, **grumpy** and **competitive**.

3 This shape is used for strong **likeable** characters who can be **thoughtful** and **sensitive**. They're usually **modest** and **supportive** of others.

4 When we think of this shape, soft and safe images appear. This shape shows friendly characters who are optimistic. These are happy characters who are sociable, **chatty** and **outgoing**.
Many famous cartoon and comic book characters are designed around this shape.

Describing personal characteristics

4 Look at characters A–D. Which adjectives would you use to describe them? Why?

5 Check the meaning of the words in bold in the text. Read the descriptions 1–4 and match pictures A–D with the descriptions.

6 Which characters have mainly positive adjectives? Which have mainly negative ones? Are there any adjectives that could be positive or negative?

7 Match the definitions with the words in bold in the text. Then think of a character from a film, book or video game for each adjective.
1. not willing to let anything prevent them from doing what they have decided to do
2. not willing to change their ideas or consider anyone else's reasons or arguments
3. kind, and showing that they consider that what other people want or need is important
4. unhappy and dissatisfied, often for no obvious reason; often complaining
5. friendly and enjoys talking to people
6. helpful and sympathetic

8 🔊 4 Listen to a podcast extract about character design. Put pictures A–D in the order in which they are mentioned.

9 What do you know about the characters in the box? Listen again. Which shape is each character?

| Superman | Super Mario | The Incredible Hulk |
| The Joker | Wreck-It Ralph | Zelda |

10 💬 Work in pairs. Complete the sentences so that they are true for you. Ask your partner about their sentences.
1. I'd say my best friend/father/sister is (…) , but he/she couldn't be described as (…) .
2. I consider myself to be (…) , but not (…) .

VIDEO SKILLS

11 🎥 Watch the video. Does the narrator believe personality types are fixed?

12 💬 Work in pairs. This video uses a lot of text on-screen. Is this useful?

1 Reading and critical thinking

A magazine article

1 Look at the photos in the article and answer the questions.
1. Describe the clothes and think about the colours. What kind of people might wear them?
2. What do you think is unusual about the lifestyles of the people in the article?

2 🔊 5 Read and listen to the article. Check your answers to exercise 1.

3 Complete the sentences with *Ella* or *Gary*.
1. (…) still only wears one colour.
2. (…) chose their colour because of a family member.
3. (…) started wearing their colour when they were a student.
4. (…) has got furniture and a vehicle in their colour.
5. (…) once received lots of gifts in their colour.

4 Are the sentences true, false or is there no information? Correct the false sentences.
1. Before she got married, Ella didn't use to wear only yellow clothes.
2. Ella chose yellow even though it didn't really suit her personality.
3. Ella is thinking about getting other yellow items, such as makeup or a car.
4. Ella often posts photos of herself on Instagram.
5. Gary now loves purple, although he didn't when he was a child.
6. Gary lost business because of his clothes.

5 Answer the questions in your own words. Give evidence for your answers.
1. How has colour been used in advertising?
2. What did Ella find hardest about dressing only in yellow?
3. Why does Ella like dressing in yellow?
4. How did so many people become interested in Ella?
5. When did Gary start wearing only purple clothes?
6. Why does Gary like the colour purple?

▶ **Subskill: Keeping a record of vocabulary**
When you record a word or phrase, it's a good idea to include pronunciation, part of speech (noun, verb, etc.), a definition and an example sentence. Adding related words is also useful.

6 Look at the vocabulary record and find the word in the text. Complete the sentences with the correct form of the word.

> **excessive** (ADJECTIVE) /ɪkˈsesɪv/
> much more than is reasonable or necessary
> The charges seemed a little excessive.
>
> excessively (ADVERB), excess (NOUN)

1. He was not (…) polite – in fact he was rather rude!
2. The shop had an (…) of cakes so they gave them away.
3. The amount of force used was (…). It wasn't necessary.

7 **Word work** Record the other words in bold in the article. Then complete sentences 1–6 with the correct form of the words.
1. Hours later, I can still see the painting clearly in my mind; it was very (…).
2. She always says 'pip pip' instead of 'goodbye'; it's her (…) phrase.
3. They always wear black clothes because they're goths. It's their (…).
4. Sam can't stop talking about politics – it's become a real (…) with him.
5. I bought three things in the sales, but my favourite (…) was a pink jacket.
6. White is often used to (…) peace.

8 💬 Work in pairs. Discuss the questions.
1. Do you think your clothes are the most important way to express yourself? Why/Why not?
2. Have you ever had a particular look? What is/was it?

CRITICAL THINKING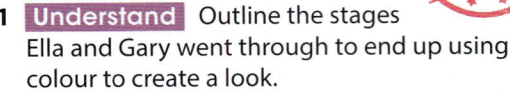

1. **Understand** Outline the stages Ella and Gary went through to end up using colour to create a look.
2. **Analyse** Think of some people you know. Do they wear one colour more than others? Can you think of reasons for this?
3. **Evaluate** Which colour is the best one for you? Give reasons for your answers.

THIS IS ME

Is it **excessive** to dress only or mainly in one colour? Could you do it? People have often used colour in advertising to **represent** brands because colour can send powerful messages at an emotional level – but what about as a personal '**trademark**'?

Ella London, who is originally from the UK but lives in Los Angeles, USA, is known as 'Miss Sunshine' because she's been wearing only yellow clothes for years. Always unconventional, she was wondering what colour wedding dress to get when her husband-to-be suggested yellow. She loved the idea because yellow was her dad's favourite colour, and the perfect colour for an optimistic and outgoing person like her.

Ella wasn't originally intending to go 'all yellow'; it happened slowly. Her first **purchase** was a top from eBay, then a friend gave her a cardigan and over the next four years, her collection grew until she was able to dress exclusively in yellow. Although shoes were the trickiest items to find, she's managed to find plenty, along with yellow make-up and accessories, yellow furniture and even a yellow car. For Ella, it's a cool way of expressing herself and she loves it when people ask about her **look**. Recently, a video about her went viral: people were fascinated by 'Miss Sunshine'. Since then she's been posting a daily photo of herself on Instagram and now has followers worldwide.

Designer Gary Card fell in love with the colour purple when he was five, although he didn't start wearing it until he was at secondary school. Initially, he changed his school jacket so that the inside of it was purple and wore purple socks. Although other students used to bully him for it, Gary was determined not to stop. After he'd qualified as a designer, he became well known for his purple outfits and having a **memorable** look was often an advantage in the design world. In his 20s, he used to only wear purple, though nowadays he mixes it with other colours.

Why purple? For Gary, it's a fascinating and mysterious colour because it's both warm and cool, and it's always in fashion. As well as clothes, he's bought purple furniture and his most expensive possessions (two portfolios for carrying artwork) are purple. He's also had some fantastic presents including 30 different purple toothbrushes from his mother.

While some people might argue that dressing in a single colour is an **obsession**, for others it's a way of life that makes them feel good. Perhaps the most important thing is to be true to yourself.

1 Grammar

Past tenses

1 Read examples a–d and match them with the tenses/structures in the box. Then answer questions 1–4.

> past continuous   past perfect simple
> past simple   used to

> a At secondary school, he changed his school jacket so that the inside of it was purple.
> b She was wondering what colour to use in the colour theme of her wedding.
> c He used to only wear purple, though nowadays he mixes it with other colours.
> d After he'd qualified, he became known for his purple outfits.

Which tense/structure do we use for … ?

1 finished past actions, states and habits, often with a past time expression
2 past habits or repeated actions and states that are no longer true
3 an action that happened before another action in the past
4 actions that were in progress at a certain time in the past, actions that continued for some time and descriptions of background events

2 💬 Work in pairs. Choose the correct option. Say if the sentences are true for you.

1 By the time I got to school this morning, I **made/had made** over ten phone calls.
2 I **wore/was wearing** a school uniform at 7:00 pm yesterday.
3 When I was a child, I **had got/used to get** obsessed with particular outfits. Once, I even **wore/used to wear** a favourite outfit to bed!
4 My best friend **bought/used to buy** some red jeans recently.
5 I **wasn't liking/didn't like** black clothes when I was younger, but now I do.

Present perfect simple and present perfect continuous

3 Read the examples and complete the rules with the correct tense.

> He's also had some fantastic presents.
> Ella's been wearing only yellow clothes for years.
> I've always worn a lot of bright colours, but recently I've been wearing more dark clothes.

1 We use the (…) when the action is unfinished and the focus is on the action or process.
2 We use the (…) to show the present result of a finished action when the focus is on the result.
3 We use the (…) to emphasise duration.

4 Complete the sentences with the correct present perfect simple or continuous form of the verbs in brackets.

1 I (…) (**do**) my homework all morning. I (…) (**finish**) my maths, but I (…) (**not do**) my history yet.
2 How long (…) (**you / know**) Sara?
3 Max (…) (**always like**) red, but recently he (…) (**wear**) more pink clothes.
4 My mum is really good at designing clothes. She (…) (**do**) it for years.

5 Complete the text with the correct form of the verbs in brackets.

> ### ZACK PINSENT
> 1 (…) you ever (…) (**wear**) any historical clothes? Zack Pinsent has. In fact, he 2 (…) (**wear**) clothes that were in fashion in the early 19th century for over ten years! When he was younger, Zack 3 (…) (**dress**) in modern clothes, but he 4 (…) (**stop**) wearing them, except for his school uniform, when he was 14 years old. Why? One day, after his family 5 (…) (**move**) home, he 6 (…) (**find**) his great-grandfather's old suits. After he 7 (…) (**try**) them on, he 8 (…) (**realise**) they suited him. Now Zack only wears historical clothes. He 9 (…) (**design**) his outfits for years now and doesn't plan to stop.

6 Answer the questions to solve the Brain teaser.

1 Jack researched personality for five years.
2 Dominic has been researching since 2014.
3 Mark used to research personality.
4 Lucia has spent some time researching, but not recently.

Who is still doing research? How do you know?

Pronunciation: /h/ ➜ p116

Vocabulary and Listening

Phrasal verbs: three-part verbs

1 Read the magazine article. Who are you most/least like? Why?

TEENS TALK: What do you think of personality quizzes?

We asked your opinions and this is what you said.

A I love them – I learn a lot about myself! I always **look out for** interesting ones to do. I'm amazed the writers haven't **run out of** ideas yet! I don't always **get round to** doing all the ones I see, though.
SONIA, 16

B Most of them are silly. I don't know how people **come up with** the ideas or how they **get away with** convincing people that the quizzes are accurate.
MARIO, 15

C They're just a bit of fun, aren't they? Should you **do away with** them? No, they're a laugh! I only ever believe the good bits, though. The last one I did said I **get on with** people – it's true, I'm really outgoing!
SAM, 18

D I don't really **go in for** them – they're a waste of time. I don't know why people **go on about** them and say they're great. They never **live up to** your expectations.
NEETA, 16

2 Match definitions 1–6 with six of the phrasal verbs in bold in exercise 1.
1 manage to do something without any bad results
2 remove something
3 be as good as what was expected or promised
4 try to find or see a particular person or thing
5 enjoy a particular thing or activity
6 do something after you have intended to do it for a long time

3 Choose the correct option. Do you agree or disagree with the sentences? Why?
1 It's easy to **come up with/get away with** original ideas.
2 I'm very organised and I never **run out of/go in for** time for things.
3 The last film I saw didn't **get round to/live up to** my expectations. It was disappointing!
4 It's important to **get on with/go on about** everyone. It isn't good to argue.
5 Schools should **look out for/do away with** homework. We need to have more free time.

Short interviews

4 🔊6 Listen to three people giving their opinions. Which three people from exercise 1 do you hear? In what order?

▶ **Subskill: Dealing with homophones**
A homophone is a word that sounds the same as another word, but has a different spelling and meaning, e.g. *where/wear, know/no, whole/hole.*

5 Choose the correct option. Then write sentences with the incorrect words.
1 I'm always looking for good personality quiz **sites/sights**.
2 For me, **they're/their** like horoscopes – you believe the good bits.
3 I was surprised to **here/hear** that some universities use them.
4 Nobody takes personality quizzes seriously, **write/right**?
5 Personality tests shouldn't be **allowed/aloud** in job interviews.
6 When people confirm your personality, **it's/its** very powerful.
7 I can't **wait/weight** to do another personality quiz.
8 I'm really **board/bored** by personality tests.

6 Listen again. Are the sentences true or false? Correct the false sentences.
1 Sam agreed completely with the results of the quiz he did yesterday.
2 He says personality tests can help you find out whether you see yourself as others see you.
3 Sonia became interested in personality tests after doing a project.
4 She was disappointed with the results of the 'Big Five' personality test.
5 Neeta thinks most online quizzes are very useful.
6 She was surprised that some companies use personality tests in interviews.

7 💬 Work in pairs. Which opinions in exercise 5 do you agree with? Why?

Pronunciation: Homophones → p116

1 Grammar

Past perfect simple and past simple

1 Choose the correct option to complete the rules.

> I found out that online quizzes had recently become really popular.
> After I'd read the results, I laughed.
> I read/had read the quiz a day before I completed it.

1 We use the past perfect simple to talk about an action that happened **after/before** another action in the past.
2 In sentences with *before* or *after*, if the past perfect action happened at a **specific/general** time in the past, we can use the past perfect or past simple as the order of events is clear.

2 Complete the sentences with the correct past simple or past perfect simple form of the verbs in brackets.

1 When my alarm (…) **(go off)** this morning, I (…) **(already get up)**.
2 I (…) **(start)** learning English when I (…) **(be)** five years old.
3 This morning, after I (…) **(have)** breakfast, I (…) **(phone)** my friend.
4 My best friend and I (…) **(never hear)** of people wearing only one colour before we (…) **(read)** about them.
5 I (…) **(miss)** the bus to school because it (…) **(leave)** by the time I got to the bus stop.

3 💬 Work in pairs. Are the sentences in exercise 2 true or false for your partner?

Past perfect simple and past perfect continuous

4 Read the examples and complete the rules with *duration*, *cause* or *past*.

> After I'd written the questions, I interviewed some people.
> I was curious because more people had been doing online tests.
> I had been doing research for a project, but I hadn't found anything interesting.

1 We use the past perfect continuous to talk about an action that started in the (…) and continued up to another time in the past.
2 With the past perfect continuous, the emphasis is on the (…) of the action and we often use it to show (…) and effect.

5 Complete the sentences with the correct past perfect simple or past perfect continuous form of the verbs in brackets.

1 John was grumpy because he (…) **(work)** hard all morning and he (…) **(not have)** breakfast.
2 Sam (…) **(study)** a lot before he did his exams and he passed them all.
3 I was happy when I found my glasses – I (…) **(look)** for them for ages.
4 Before Lucy and I were neighbours, we (…) **(know)** each other since we were four.
5 It (…) **(snow)** for hours. By the time we went inside, we (…) **(build)** a huge snowman.

6 Complete the text with the correct past simple, past perfect simple or past perfect continuous form of the verbs in brackets.

> The first watch that could download information from computers **1** (…) **(appear)** in 1994, but scientists **2** (…) **(try)** to improve watch technology since the first digital watch **3** (…) **(become)** available in 1972. Years later, a company called Pebble **4** (…) **(change)** everything. They **5** (…) **(work)** on a new smartwatch that could make phone calls, use apps and listen to music for some time, and they **6** (…) **(use)** crowdfunding to produce it. Their watch, the Pebble, **7** (…) **(come)** out in 2013. Before that, there **8** (…) **(be)** many attempts to create a truly 'smart' watch. Steve Mann **9** (…) **(design)** an early form in 1998, but it **10** (…) **(not have)** many of the features today's smartwatches have.

7 Complete the text with the correct form of the verbs in brackets.

GRAMMAR ROUND-UP
1 2 3 4 5 6 7 8

> Imagine you **1** (…) **(meet)** someone at a party last week. You might forget their name, but you'd probably remember their face. Although it is a complex thing to do, humans **2** (…) **(always be able)** to recognise other people's faces. Scientists first **3** (…) **(start)** developing computer programs to identify human faces in the 1960s and they **4** (…) **(work)** on these programs ever since, though they **5** (…) **(not succeed)** in developing a 100% accurate program yet. A few years ago, officials in Boston Airport **6** (…) **(stop)** using facial recognition technology after they **7** (…) **(use)** it for about three months, as it only had a 61.4% success rate. Recently, new 3D technology **8** (…) **(have)** better results and it is now being used in cities across the world.

Real-world speaking

Solving shopping issues

1 🎥 Watch the video. What solution do they find for the problem?

2 Watch again. Complete gaps 1–4 in the dialogue.

3 Watch again. Which Key phrases do you hear?

Shop assistant
> Good morning. Can I help you?

Owen
> Yes, I'd like to **1** (…) this jacket. I bought it here two days ago.

Shop assistant
> Of course. Can I ask why you're returning it?

Owen
> It's really badly made! When I tried it on at home, the sleeve almost came off.

Shop assistant
> I see. Have you got the receipt?

Owen
> I'm afraid I've lost the receipt.

Shop assistant
> I'm sorry, but I can't give you a **2** (…) without a receipt. I can **3** (…) the jacket in the same size or in a different size if you prefer.

Owen
> No, definitely not.

Shop assistant
> In that case, you can exchange it for something else. Would you like to choose something now?

Owen
> I haven't really got time now.

Shop assistant
> No problem. I can give you a **4** (…) and you can use it any time in the next six months.

Owen
> OK, thanks.

4 Create your own dialogue. Follow the steps in the Skills boost.

SKILLS BOOST

THINK
You need to return an item to a shop. Make notes about your reasons.

PREPARE
Prepare a dialogue. Remember to use the Key phrases for solving shopping issues.

PRACTISE
Practise your dialogue.

PERFORM
Act out your dialogue for the class or record it and play it to the class.

5 **Peer review** Listen to your classmates and answer the questions.
1 Were they successful in resolving the issue?
2 Which Key phrases did they use?

Key phrases

Asking about the issue
Can I ask why you are returning it?
Have you got the receipt?

Issues
I'd like to return … / I'm afraid there's a problem with …
(It) broke/shrank/came off … / (It)'s badly made.
(It) doesn't fit properly / (It) isn't right.
I can't give you a refund without a receipt.
I'm afraid I've lost the receipt.

Solutions
I can give you a refund or replace it for you.
You can exchange it for something else.
I can give you a credit note.

Real-world grammar

I **bought** it here two days ago.
I'm afraid I**'ve lost** the receipt.

Phrasebook → p122

Writing

SOMEONE I KNOW ...

1 Sara might not be somebody you notice immediately, but she's definitely someone you want to know better. We met one evening, when it was absolutely freezing and completely dark – I'd missed my usual bus home and was waiting nervously at the bus stop. Sara was there too, so we started chatting. That was two years ago and we've been friends since then.

2 Sara's short and slim with brown eyes. She's chatty and likeable, and gets on well with everyone, although she is a little shy. Once you get to know her, you realise she's extremely supportive of all her friends and she's really thoughtful. She's always ready to help and listen to your problems. She can be slightly grumpy if she's hungry or tired, but she's usually enthusiastic and funny.

3 One incident with Sara stands out in my memory. A group of us had been playing beach volleyball all afternoon, so we were really exhausted. Suddenly, I realised I'd lost my favourite necklace. We searched everywhere. Finally, the others left, except Sara. She was determined to find it, although I'd given up hope. An hour later, while I was complaining, she laughed and held up my necklace! I'll never forget that.

4 I am delighted that I met Sara and proud that she's my friend. She's one of the kindest and most optimistic people I've ever met – and definitely an interesting character!

Marina Moss

A description of a person

1 Read the description. How long has the writer known Sara?

2 Read the description again and match paragraphs 1–4 with descriptions a–d.
   a a detailed description of the person, including a short physical description
   b a short introduction, including how you know the person and a general description of the person
   c a brief conclusion
   d an anecdote that tells you more about the person

▶ **Subskill: Gradable and non-gradable adjectives + adverbs**

Before gradable adjectives, use: *a little, extremely, fairly, rather, slightly, really, quite, very.*
Before extreme or absolute adjectives, use: *absolutely, completely, really, totally.*

3 Read the description again and find:
   1 four examples of adverbs + gradable adjectives
   2 three examples of adverbs + extreme or absolute adjectives
   3 an adverb that can go with any type of adjective

4 Choose the correct option and then complete the sentences with your own ideas.
   1 David is **extremely/absolutely** hilarious; he often (…) .
   2 He's **quite/completely** tall and he's got **totally/very** short (…) .
   3 He's a **really/very** wonderful friend because (…) .
   4 He can occasionally be **a little/totally** stubborn and **completely/slightly** pessimistic, but (…) .
   5 Although he's **really/fairly** terrible at sports, he (…) .
   6 I think that David is **a quite/an absolutely** fantastic person and I (…) .

5 Complete the anecdote with suitable words from exercise 4.

I remember one time we went camping with my friends. When we arrived, it was raining heavily and we got **1** (…) soaked putting our **2** (…) old tent up. Then we discovered we'd left most of our food behind. I was **3** (…) furious, but Serena just laughed. She's **4** (…) creative with food and **5** (…) sensible, and she was determined to have fun. She quickly cooked something with the ingredients we had – it was a/an **6** (…) interesting meal and **7** (…) delicious! It was a/an **8** (…) unforgettable experience.

6 Find all the adjectives in the text in exercise 1. Write your own sentences about people you know with the adjectives and with the adverbs in the box.

> absolutely   extremely   quite   rather   very

*My best friend is **very** supportive and **extremely** thoughtful.*

7 Write a description of an interesting person. Follow the steps in the Skills boost.

SKILLS BOOST

THINK
Choose a person to write about. It can be someone you know well, an acquaintance or an imaginary person.
Make notes about the person. Include how you met them, details of their appearance and character, and an anecdote about them.
Note down any useful vocabulary from the model text or unit.

PREPARE
Look at the paragraph plan in exercise 2 and organise your notes into four paragraphs.
Look at the adverbs in the Subskill and decide which to use and where to use them.

WRITE
Write your description. Use the model to help you.

CHECK
Read your description and answer the questions.
1 Have you used a variety of the tenses covered in the unit?
2 Have you used personality adjectives and adjectives describing characteristics?
3 Did you make and follow a paragraph plan?
4 Have you used adverbs with gradable, extreme and absolute adjectives?

8 **Peer review** Exchange your description with another student. Answer the questions.
1 Was the description clear and well organised?
2 Has your partner included all the things in the checklist?
3 Did it make you want to meet this person? Why/Why not?

QUICK REVIEW 1

Grammar

Past tenses
We use the past simple to talk about finished actions or states in the past.
*He **started** wearing only purple clothes.*
We use the past continuous to talk about actions in progress at a time in the past and to set the scene for descriptions.
*While I **was waiting** for the bus, my friend arrived.*
*The sun **was shining** and everyone **was feeling** happy.*
We use *used to* to talk about past habits or states that are no longer true.
*I **used to be** very stubborn, but I'm more flexible these days.*
*They **used to wear** lots of different colours, but now they only wear blue.*

Present perfect simple and present perfect continuous
We use the present perfect simple to talk about actions or states that started in the past and continue in the present. We use the present perfect continuous to emphasise duration and for repeated actions when the focus is on the action or process.
*I**'ve lived** here for ten years.*
*He**'s been making** a video. He**'s filmed** it, but he **hasn't edited** it yet.*
*We**'ve been going** on holiday to Spain for years.*

Past perfect simple and past simple
We use the past perfect simple to talk about an event that had happened before another event in the past. We use the past simple for a more recent event.
*The film **had** already **started** when we **arrived** at the cinema.*

Past perfect continuous
We use the past perfect continuous to talk about an action that started in the past and continued up to another time in the past, to emphasise the duration of an action before another action in the past and to talk about cause and effect.
*We **had been walking** for hours before we reached the lake.*
*My face was red because I **had been running**.*

Vocabulary

🔊7 **Personal qualities**
confident, creative, enthusiastic, generous, hard-working, patient, polite, reliable, sensible, sociable

🔊8 **Describing personal characteristics**
aggressive, arrogant, chatty, clumsy, competitive, cruel, determined, grumpy, likeable, modest, outgoing, selfish, sensitive, stubborn, supportive, thoughtful

🔊9 **Phrasal verbs: three-part verbs**
come up with, do away with, get away with, get on with, get round to, go in for, go on about, live up to, look out for, run out of

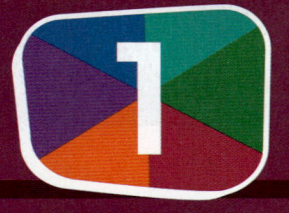

1 Project

WDYT? (What do you think?)

What makes you the person you are?

TASK: Create a poster about your personal identity including a self-portrait and a description of yourself.

Learning outcomes

1 I can make a poster about personal identity.

2 I can use appropriate grammar and vocabulary from the unit.

3 I can use visuals to communicate my ideas.

Graphic organiser → Project planner p118

1 Watch a video of a student presenting his poster about personal identity. What fun fact about himself does he include?

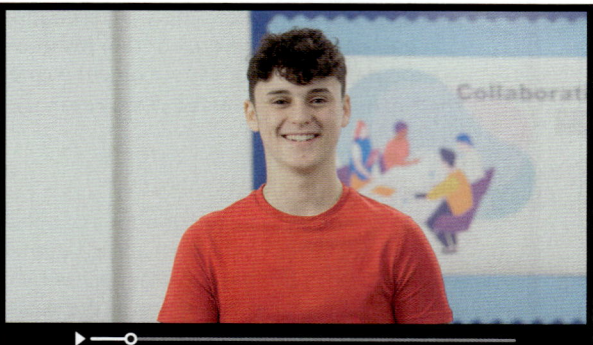

STEP 1: THINK

2 In what order do you think a–e should appear in a description of personal identity?

a a fun fact

b a description of your appearance and personality

c a brief introduction about yourself

d a personal anecdote

e your hobbies and interests

3 Read the Model project and check your guesses.

STEP 2: PLAN

4 Look at the start of Jake's mind map and the Model project. What information is missing?

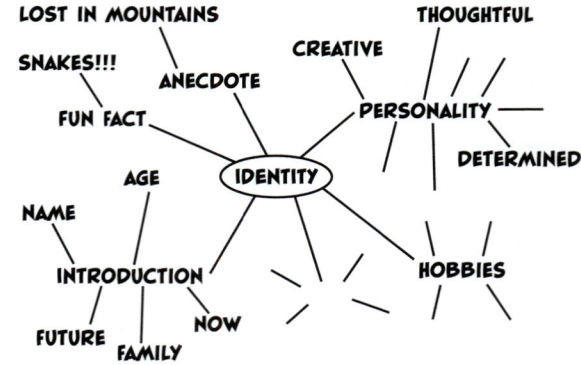

5 Read the *How to …* tips on p118 and create a mind map for your poster.

STEP 3: CREATE

6 Work in pairs. Read the tips in the Super skills box and practise saying the Key phrases with a partner.

COMMUNICATION SUPER SKILLS

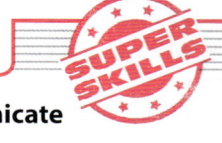

Using visuals to communicate your ideas

Tips

Decide what you want to communicate.

Choose or create visuals that best represent your ideas in an attractive and interesting way.

Key phrases

I used (images/drawings) to represent …

I put (the personality adjectives) here because I wanted to suggest that …

I wanted to show that (my interests are things I think about), so I …

I used (these pictures) because I thought they were (clear and attractive).

I thought that (using colours) like this was a powerful way to (show my personality).

This represents/gives the message …

Grammar and Vocabulary → Quick review p21

Model project

1 Fact file
Age: 16
From: Newcastle, England
Family: mother, father, two sisters
Occupation: student
Career aspiration: advertising

WHO AM I?

2 I'm quite tall and I've got fairly long dark brown hair, which is a little wavy. My eyes are brown. I'm really creative and my friends say I'm always coming up with rather interesting ideas – I haven't run out of them yet! I'm very sociable and I get on with most people, although I can be quite shy with new people. I'd say I'm determined, reliable and thoughtful, too. I can be a little lazy and I don't always get round to finishing things I've started. People have said I can be a bit stubborn sometimes!

3 My passions are art and music, and I can sing and play the guitar. I also love drawing and painting. I enjoy going to the cinema or hanging out with friends.

4 I don't really go in for sports, but I love being outside – as long as there are no snakes. They absolutely terrify me!

5 Once, I got lost on a mountain when I was younger. I'd been walking there with my family and I went down to the river to get more water. When I returned, I took the wrong path. Luckily, my phone was still working, so I phoned my dad and we managed to meet up – two hours later!

OPTIMISTIC DETERMINED THOUGHTFUL GENEROUS SOCIABLE LAZY KIND CREATIVE OUTGOING RELIABLE ENTHUSIASTIC STUBBORN SHY CHATTY PATIENT

7 Create your poster.

8 Prepare and practise your presentation. Refer to the visuals, and use the tips and Key phrases in the Super skills box.

STEP 4: PRESENT

9 Give your presentation to the class and answer any questions.

10 *Peer review* Listen to the other presentations and answer the questions.
  1 Which poster(s) do you think explain the person's identity best? Why?
  2 Which poster(s) do you think have the most creative artwork? Give your reasons.

 FINAL REFLECTION

1 The task
Were your mind map and poster well organised and complete?

2 Super skill
Did you use visuals to communicate your ideas in an interesting and attractive way?

3 Language
Did you use new language from this unit? Give examples.

Beyond the task
Is it important to know your own strengths and weaknesses? When is this useful?

2 Welcome to the future!

WDYT? (What do you think?)

What changes would you like to see in the future?

Vocabulary: describing products; changes; expressions with *get*

Grammar: future tenses; future continuous and future perfect; future time expressions

Reading: a scientific report about changes in everyday life in the future

Listening: an informal conversation about robots

Speaking: organising an event

Writing: a product review

Project: a presentation on changes in the future

FACING THE FUTURE

Do you **welcome** new challenges or do you find them **a real struggle**?

1 The fourth industrial revolution will bring **mind-blowing** changes in areas like artificial intelligence and nanotechnology. Will you be able to **let go** of the past and **embrace** the new?

NO What's wrong with old-fashioned things anyway?

YES Sure! I can **adapt** to any **new circumstances**!

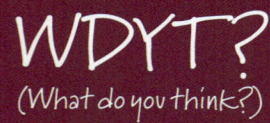
Video skills p25

Real-world speaking p31

Project pp34–35

Describing products

1 Look at the words in the box. Which adjectives form a negative with prefixes *un-* or *im-*? What is the opposite of the others?

> comfortable   easy-to-use   handy/useful   high quality   innovative
> practical   reasonable   reliable   wearable   well-made

2 10 Listen to Oscar talking to Mia about useful devices and answer the questions.
1 What's her latest device?
2 Which device would Oscar like to see in the future?
3 Which of the words in exercise 1 do they use?

3 Work in pairs. Discuss your favourite devices and the ones you would like to use in the future.

Vocabulary 2

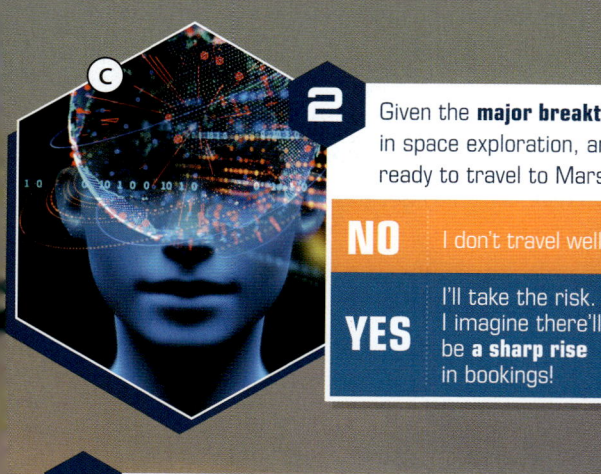

2 Given the **major breakthroughs** in space exploration, are you ready to travel to Mars?

NO I don't travel well anyway.

YES I'll take the risk. I imagine there'll be **a sharp rise** in bookings!

3 Are you **eager** to get your motorbike or driving licence?

NO With the age of driverless vehicles **fast approaching**, is it worth it?

YES I may still need to take control of the vehicle if something **unexpected** happens.

4 **Advances** in DNA technology are great for the safety of our society.

NO This technology **is evolving** rapidly; who knows what scientists will do next and at what cost?

YES It means we can catch criminals more easily through fingerprints or skin particles.

Mainly NO
Enjoy the past while you can, but remember that you can't slow down progress.

Mainly YES
You're obviously thinking about the future and it looks like you'll enjoy it!

Changes

4 Check the meanings of the words and phrases in bold in the quiz. Then match questions 1–4 with images A–D.

5 Work in pairs. Do the quiz. Compare your answers with your partner. Do you agree with the conclusions?

6 Copy and complete the table with the words in the quiz.

Nouns	Verbs	Adjectives
a (real) struggle	welcome	mind-blowing

7 Complete the sentences with the words in the box.

> fast   major   new   real   sharp

1 I find switching over to a new mobile device a (…) struggle.
2 I'm sure we'll see a (…) rise in the use of electric vehicles.
3 Quantum computers will be a (…) breakthrough – computers will be faster than ever.
4 Some people say the age of digital money is (…) approaching.
5 With so many changes, we'll all have to adapt to (…) circumstances.

8 Complete the questions with words from the quiz in the correct form.

1 Are you (…) to try a driverless vehicle? Why/Why not?
2 Do you know anyone who finds learning to use new technology a real (…) ? Is it easy to help them?
3 How would you like mobile devices (…) in the future?
4 People say that there have been some (…) changes in technology this century. Do you agree?
5 What do you think the next technological (…) will be? Will you (…) it? Why/Why not?

9 Work in pairs. Ask and answer the questions in exercise 8.

VIDEO SKILLS

10 Watch the video. What is it about?

11 Work in pairs. Discuss the questions.
1 This video uses a timeline throughout. Why?
2 There are lots of images in this video. Why do you think this is?

Pronunciation: /æ/, /ɑː/ and /eɪ/ → p116

25

2 Reading and critical thinking

A scientific report

1 💬 **Work in pairs. How do you think these things will be done in the future?**
  a farming and producing food
  b communicating with each other
  c diagnosing and treating illnesses

▶ **Subskill: Predicting content**
Use the title, photos and any general comprehension questions to predict the content of a text. Then read the text to check your predictions.

2 Look at the title of the report and the photos. Read the sentences. Which option do you think is correct?
  1 By the middle of this century, the world population will have reached …
    a just under 10 billion people.
    b almost 15 billion.
  2 … that indoor crops are getting enough light and food to grow.
    a Farmers will check
    b Computers will check
  3 Indoor farming is likely to be … to the environment than traditional farming.
    a more harmful   b less harmful
  4 The writer … we'll be able to keep in touch with our friends without a physical device.
    a isn't certain whether   b is sure that
  5 Microdevices will be able to treat patients … of humans.
    a without the help   b with the help

3 🔊 11 **Read and listen to the report. Check your predictions in exercise 2 and find evidence to support them.**

4 Word work Match the definitions to the words in bold in the report.
  1 pieces of metal that can stick to other metal objects
  2 the smallest parts of a living structure that can operate as independent units
  3 objects that doctors put into someone's body during a medical operation
  4 given a natural or chemical substance in order to grow
  5 tubes inside humans through which blood flows
  6 take care of an animal, sometimes when farming

5 Complete the sentences with the correct form of some of the words in exercise 4.
  1 We've used a (…) to get the key out from behind the cupboard.
  2 My grandpa's tomatoes are (…) with organic waste from our kitchen.
  3 Red blood (…) carry oxygen around our bodies.
  4 Our neighbours have always (…) chickens in their garden.
  5 Would you welcome a mobile phone (…) behind your ear or in your arm?

6 Read the report again and answer the questions.
  1 In what ways will indoor farming have less of an impact on the environment?
  2 How will scientists create meat in the laboratory?
  3 What are the main differences between the smartphones we use now and the wearable screens we may use in the future?
  4 Why are the robot birds such a major breakthrough?

7 💬 **Work in pairs. Answer the questions.**
  1 Would you eat vegetables grown vertically in water?
  2 Which of the new kinds of phones would you prefer? Why?
  3 In your opinion, is research in nanotechnology important?

CRITICAL THINKING

1 **Remember** Write one sentence to describe each of the three advances in the report.
2 **Analyse** Which are the most useful? Why?
3 **Create** Design your own wearable screen. What functions does it have? Do you think wearable screens will have a positive or negative impact on our lives?

INNOVATIONS THAT WILL ROCK OUR WORLD

In this week's report, we're going to have a look at some rapidly evolving technologies and consider how they might change our lives forever.

High-rise farming and food production

The United Nations predicts that the world population will have reached 9.8 billion by 2050, but our farmland will probably not be able to support the necessary food production. A solution may be to grow crops and raise animals on top of skyscrapers or, alternatively, develop indoor farming using artificial light. The crops will be grown in vertical containers of water rather than soil, and then **fertilised** by the waste products from animals. Computers will control the process automatically, making sure the plants get the right balance of food and light. This means we'll enjoy a variety of food all year round without relying on the weather or damaging the land further. In the same way, creating meat and seafood by growing **cells** from the muscle of an animal in the laboratory is a fast-approaching reality. This lab-grown or 'clean' meat could mean that we no longer need to **raise** animals on farms. Both advances will help to reduce the impact farming has on the environment.

Communication via wearable screens

You're meeting a friend in town in 15 minutes, but you've missed the bus. The next bus doesn't leave for ten minutes. You're going to be late again. In 2040, you probably won't need to reach for your smartphone: you'll contact your friend through a screen projected onto your arm. What makes us think that? There has been a sharp rise in wearable phones. They're an improvement on smartwatches because you can take calls, swipe through your favourite apps and tap to select one from your wrist. They don't only have voice recognition, but also gesture recognition – you can wave your finger to scroll up or down. And one day, perhaps we'll be able to replace devices with small **implants** under our skin.

Microdevice treatment

Scientists in Switzerland have created a tiny device which looks something like an origami bird. This mind-blowing bird is just a few micrometres long, so it can only be seen under a microscope. Through the use of **magnets**, it can be programmed to move its wings, bend its neck, move its head, hover and turn. How will that improve our lives? Well, in a not-too-distant future, perhaps doctors will be programming these birds to perform medical tasks in the body. For example, one of them could fly through our **blood vessels** killing cancer cells.

The longer read → Resource centre

2 Grammar

Future tenses

1 Read examples a–f and match them with the words in the box.

> be going to   present continuous   present simple   will

> a You've missed the bus. You're going to be late again.
> b In 2040, you probably won't need to reach for your smartphone.
> c I've missed the bus. I'll let my friend know.
> d The next bus doesn't leave for ten minutes.
> e You're meeting a friend in town in 15 minutes.
> f In this report, we're going to have a look at some rapidly evolving technologies.

2 Which future form do we use to talk about these things? Use the examples in exercise 1 to help you.

1. a timetable or programme
2. a future arrangement, often with a date, time and place
3. a future plan or intention which is already decided (often without an exact date)
4. general predictions about the future, often with *I think*, *I hope*, *I'm sure*, *probably*, *definitely*, etc.
5. predictions about the future for which we can see some evidence now
6. a decision which we make at the moment of speaking

3 Choose the correct option.

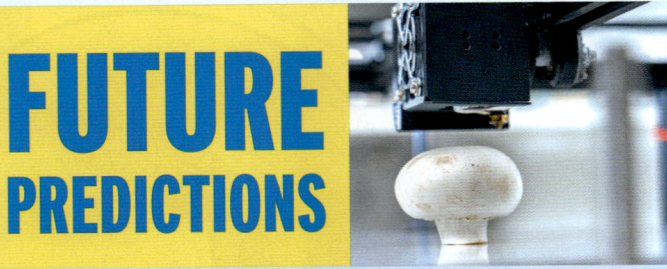

We predict that there **1 is being/will be** a major breakthrough in 3D printing and that you **2 can/will be able to** print your own dinner. Imagine you've just found out that one of your friends is a vegetarian and that they **3 are arriving/arrive** for dinner soon. The local supermarket **4 closes/will close** in ten minutes. In the future, having to run to the shops **5 is/will be** a thing of the past. You **6 are being able/will be able** to print another meal in minutes!

7 Are you going/Do you go camping next weekend? Do you want to know if it's **8 raining/going to rain** on Saturday? In the not-too-distant future, your smart mirror **9 is showing/will show** you the weather forecast and it **10 is also checking/will also check** whether you're well enough to go!

4 Complete the dialogue with the correct future form of the verbs in brackets. There may be more than one possible answer.

> 1 (…) you (…) (**do**) anything tomorrow?

> Rob's band 2 (…) (**play**) in the evening. Why?

> I 3 (…) (**go**) to the Science Museum. There 4 (…) (**be**) an exhibition on about how advances in technology 5 (…) (**change**) our lives forever. My brother says they've got an amazing VR experience.

> I've never tried virtual reality! I 6 (…) (**not / do**) anything in the morning. I 7 (…) (**go**) with you.

> Let's get the bus which 8 (…) (**leave**) at 9:00 am.

> OK. I 9 (…) (**bring**) sandwiches for lunch if you like.

> Good idea! Can you make enough for three? Sam 10 (…) (**come**), too.

5 Complete the questions with a suitable future form. Use your own ideas.

1. (…) you (…) anything tomorrow?
2. (…) you (…) over the holidays?
3. (…) you (…) when you leave school?
4. Do you think you (…) in the future?
5. (…) in the next century?

6 💬 Work in pairs. Predict your partner's answers to the questions in exercise 5. Ask and answer the questions.

7 Answer the question to solve the Brain teaser.

You're going to spend the night on a desert island and it's getting dark. You've got a box of matches, some driftwood, a candle and some newspaper.

What will you light first?

Expressions with *get*

1 Work in pairs. How do we use robots in our daily lives? Make a list. Then read the short article. Did you include any of these uses?

THE EVOLUTION OF ROBOTS

There are millions of robots on Earth and they are rapidly **getting more sophisticated**. So, are our lives **getting better** as a result? Look at these examples and decide for yourself!

REMOTE LEARNING
When a child or young adult with a long-term illness is unable to **get to class**, AV1 robots can take their place instead. The robot sits in the lesson and **gets information**. Using an app on their mobile device to control the robot, the student at home can listen, look around and even take part.

DANGEROUS PLACES
NASA is **getting ready** to send their robot Valkyrie to Mars to help prepare for the arrival of humans. Unlike robots before her, she can walk in a similar way to humans, so she'll be able to **get out of** the spacecraft on her own and take the first steps on the planet.

2 Look at the words with *get* in bold in the text. Replace them with the correct form of words in the box.

attend   become   improve
leave   prepare   receive

3 Work in pairs. Choose the correct option to complete the questions. Then ask and answer.

1 Have you ever had a toy robot? Did you get rid **up/over/of** it?
2 Would you like a robot to go to class for you if you were getting **over/through/on** an illness?
3 What are the top three things that get **in/on/with** your nerves?
4 When was the last time you got **into/on/around** trouble? What happened?
5 How often do you get **out of/away/about** doing the housework? How do you manage it?
6 Are you going to get **in/down to/with** studying as soon as you get home?

Vocabulary and Listening 2

An informal conversation

4 🔊 12 Listen to Rob and Tania talking about robots. Answer the questions.
1 Who is excited about this new technology?
2 Who's a little uneasy?

5 Answer the questions. Then listen again and check your answers.
1 What can an AV1 robot do?
2 What happens in the TV series *Lost in Space*?
3 How can drones be used effectively?
4 Why does Tania mention the Industrial Revolution?
5 According to Tania, will robots ever be able to have feelings like humans?

▶ **Subskill: Understanding the speaker's attitude**

Listening to the way the speaker says something will help you to understand a rapid conversation.

6 🔊 13 Listen to five extracts from the dialogue. Match extracts 1–5 with emotions in the box. There is one emotion you do not need.

amused   annoyed   bored
excited   uneasy   upset

7 Listen again. Match the emotions from exercise 6 with reasons a–f. There is one reason you do not need.

a that their friend hasn't understood something properly
b about what robots may end up doing
c about a piece of news
d that their friend doesn't appear to embrace change
e robots will take over the world
f with an argument that has been used before

8 Work in pairs. Discuss the questions.
1 Will robots ever control the world? In what ways?
2 What rules will we need to protect ourselves?

Pronunciation: Intonation → p116

2 Grammar

Future continuous and future perfect

1 Read the examples and answer the questions.

Future continuous
Will we **be taking** our orders from them?
Robots **will be doing** that for us.
We **won't be going** to class.

Future perfect
Will robots **have taken** control by then?
We'll **have forgotten** how to speak to real people.
We **won't have got** rid of classrooms completely.

1 How do we form the future continuous and the future perfect?
2 Which one do we use to talk about actions that … ?
   a will be complete before a specific time in the future
   b will be in progress at a specific time in the future

2 Read the sentence pairs. Complete sentence a with the future continuous and sentence b with the future perfect.

By 2050 …

1 a We (…) **(get)** together with our friends to try new types of fish like jellyfish.
  b More common types of edible fish like cod and tuna (…) **(die out)**.

2 a There'll be robots on the football pitch, but they (…) **(not play)**. They'll be the referees.
  b A team of robots (…) **(not beat)** your country's national team in a World Cup match.

3 a Schools (…) **(not teach)** kids how to read and write. Kids (…) **(learn)** how to explain their ideas to a computer so it can record them.
  b Many people (…) **(not learn)** how to read or write. Their computers will be able to do this for them in thousands of different languages.

3 Work in pairs. Discuss how many of these predictions you think will come true. Would you embrace these changes?

4 Complete the sentences with the future continuous or future perfect form of the verbs in brackets.

1 My friends and I (…) **(play)** an important match at ten o'clock on Saturday.
2 I (…) **(relax)** by the sea this time next week.
3 My cousin (…) **(win)** an important competition by the time she's 18.
4 My best friend (…) **(study)** at university in two years' time.
5 I (…) **(travel)** around the world before I'm 30.

Future time expressions

5 Copy and complete the table with the time expressions from exercise 4.

Future continuous	Future perfect
at 6:30 pm	by 6:30

6 Work in pairs. Ask and answer questions about these topics.
- sport
- travel
- entertainment
- school and university

7 Complete the text with the correct past or future form of the verbs in brackets.

GRAMMAR ROUND-UP
1 2 3 4 5 6 7 8

From Science Fiction to Science Fact

When Jules Verne **1** (…) **(publish)** *From the Earth to the Moon* in 1865, no other writer before him **2** (…) **(go)** into such scientific detail about a journey to space. In fact, these details **3** (…) **(come)** close to predicting the Apollo 11 launch in 1969. Since Apollo 11, the Russian space agency **4** (…) **(send)** tourists into space and more companies **5** (…) **(probably / do)** the same soon.

In 1895, H. G. Wells **6** (…) **(write)** about a group of inventors who **7** (…) **(sit)** around a dining room table. Their host **8** (…) **(start)** to talk about time being the fourth dimension and later, he told them about travelling in time. After reading it, I have been wondering about these questions: **9** (…) we (…) **(travel)** through time in 50 years' time? And **10** (…) we (…) **(prevent)** a disaster by travelling back in time to fix it by the end of this century?

Real-world speaking 2

★ 10th Grade ★
MOVIE STARS PARTY
Sat 24th November 6:00 pm
Ben's Burgers, Smith Street

Organising an event

1 🎥 Watch the video and find three mistakes in the invitation.

2 Watch again. Complete gaps 1–6 in the dialogue.

3 Watch again. Which of the Key phrases do you hear?

Liam: OK, we need to **1** (…) on a date for the end of semester party.

Emma: Didn't we say the first Saturday in December?

Liam: Won't we be taking exams then?

Emma: No, we'll be done by then.

Liam: Great! Who's going to make a **2** (…) for a place?

Emma: Paul mentioned the pizza place would **3** (…) free. Do you want to go there?

Liam: But we went there last year and the year before. Can't we go somewhere else?

Emma: Like where? Every year we **4** (…) about trying a new place. What's wrong with the pizza place anyway?

Liam: I guess you're right. Will we have to **5** (…) up like movie stars again? Can we at least change the theme?

Emma: To what? A movie star theme is easy.

Liam: How about a futuristic theme for a change?

Emma: You're on! Let's **6** (…) what the others say.

4 Create your own dialogue. Follow the steps in the Skills boost.

SKILLS BOOST

THINK
Think of an event which would appeal to your friends and create an invitation. Look at the model invitation to help you.

PREPARE
Remember to include phrases to make suggestions, negotiate and agree or disagree.

PRACTISE
Practise your dialogue.

PERFORM
Act out your dialogue for the class or record it and play it to your class.

5 **Peer review** Listen to your classmates and answer the questions.
1 Would you like to attend their event?
2 Which Key phrases did they use?

Key phrases

Making suggestions
Didn't we say … ?
Shall we go for that then?
Can't we go somewhere else? / Can we at least … ?
How about / What about … (for a change)?

Negotiating
Won't we be … then?   Like where/what/who?
Who's going to … ?   What's wrong with … anyway?

Agreeing and disagreeing
You're on!   I guess you're right.
I'm not so sure about that.

🇺🇸 US → UK 🇬🇧

Won't we be **taking** exams then? (US) →
Won't we be **doing** exams then? (UK)

Phrasebook → p122

31

2 Writing

TECHWORLD
HOME NEWS REVIEWS MORE ▼ SUBSCRIBE

Home > Reviews > HD237xe

HD237xe ★★★★★

I've just purchased the HD237xe wireless model online. Although I find it much easier to get down to doing my homework with music in the background, my sister doesn't and I was getting fed up with having to turn it down when my family was home. I'll also be able to watch TV series on my tablet without disturbing my sister.

What I love about them is they're extremely easy to use and the sound quality is outstanding. Even though they're lightweight, they feel really strong. They're stylish with an adjustable leather headband that doesn't squeeze your head. The comfortable black and gold over-ear pads definitely won't make your ears sweaty, even after hours of use.

However, there are a couple of annoying things. Despite being able to listen to music with excellent sound quality, the battery drains fast and they take longer than average to charge. You can easily get round this by planning ahead. If you aren't going to be near an electricity socket for the day, you'll need to fully charge them the night before.

In spite of the negative points, I would definitely recommend these to music lovers. They are great if you are looking for a reasonably priced model with a great design. I'd consider getting a battery pack and spare cable for charging on the go, though.

TECHWORLD REVIEWS WANTED
Have you bought a technological device recently? Why don't you write a review about it for our readers? Don't forget to describe the good and bad points, and who you'd recommend it for. We'll publish the best reviews in next month's edition.

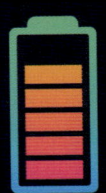

A product review

1 How often do you read reviews before you buy something? Which of the factors influence you when buying a product?
- design
- quality
- price
- a different factor

2 Read the advert from an online magazine. What is it asking for? What information do you need to include?

3 Read the review. Can you guess what technological device it is reviewing? Would you buy the device? Why/Why not?

4 Read the review again and complete the paragraph plan. Does the review mention everything in the advert?

Paragraph 1: *Describe what it is, what it does and where and when you bought it.*
Paragraph 2: (…)
Paragraph 3: (…)
Paragraph 4: (…)

5 Find the expressions used at the start of each paragraph in the review. Match expressions a–d with paragraphs 1–4.
a All things considered *4*
b On the plus side
c The downsides are
d I recently bought

▶ **Subskill: Connectors of contrast**

We can use words like *although, even though, however, in spite of* and *despite* to introduce a contrast and connect our ideas. *Although* and *though* have the same meaning, but *though* is less formal and it can be used at the end of a sentence.

6 Find six connectors of contrast in the review. What follows each one: a noun, an -*ing* form or a clause?

1 *although – a clause*

7 Rewrite the sentences with the words in brackets.

1. This wireless speaker is easy to use, but it's rather expensive. **(although)**
2. This phone is too big to fit in your pocket, but it takes amazing photos. **(despite)**
3. In spite of looking a little old-fashioned, the tablet is extremely reliable. **(even though)**
4. My smartwatch is a welcome device, but it is a real struggle to use. **(in spite of)**
5. This power bank is useful in some circumstances. However, it takes a long time to charge. **(though)**

8 Read the advert again. Then write a review for the online magazine. Follow the steps in the Skills boost.

SKILLS BOOST

THINK
Read the advert and review carefully again and choose one of these technological devices: a phone, a games console or a camera. Make notes about what it is and does, its good and bad points and your recommendation. Don't forget to introduce some contrasts and connect your ideas.

PREPARE
Use the paragraph plan in exercise 4 to organise your notes and choose an appropriate sentence beginning for each paragraph.

WRITE
Write your review, but don't include the name of the device. Use the model to help you.

CHECK
Read your review and answer the questions.
1. Have you organised your review into logical paragraphs?
2. Have you begun each paragraph with an appropriate expression?
3. Have you used connectors of contrast?
4. Have you used some of the vocabulary and grammar from this unit?

9 **Peer review** Exchange your review with a partner. Answer the questions.
1. Can you guess the technological device they are reviewing?
2. Does the review persuade you to buy the device? Why/Why not?
3. Do you think it is more convincing than your own review? Why/Why not?

QUICK REVIEW 2

Grammar

Future tenses

Predictions
We use *will* for general predictions.
You**'ll contact** your friend through a screen projected onto your wrist.
We use *be going to* for predictions with some evidence in the present.
You**'re going to be** late again.

Plans and intentions
We use the present simple for timetables.
The next bus **doesn't leave** for ten minutes.
We use the present continuous for future arrangements, often with a date, time and place.
You**'re meeting** a friend in town in 15 minutes.
We use *be going to* for future plans or intentions which are already planned.
We**'re going to have a look** at some of the technologies.
We use *will* for future plans that are decided at the moment of speaking.
Thanks for reminding me! I**'ll phone** her.

Future continuous and Future perfect

Future continuous
We use the future continuous to talk about actions that will be in progress at a specific time in the future.
Will we **be taking** our orders from them?
Robots **will be doing** that for us.
We **won't be going** to class.

Future perfect
We use the future perfect to talk about actions that will be complete before a specific time in the future.
Will robots **have taken** control by then?
We**'ll have forgotten** how to speak to real people.
We **won't have got** rid of classrooms completely.

Vocabulary

🔊 14 **Describing products**
badly-made, comfortable, difficult-to-use, easy to use, expensive, handy, hard-to-use, high quality, impractical, innovative, low quality, old-fashioned, practical, reasonable, reliable, uncomfortable, unreliable, unwearable, useful, useless, wearable, well-made

🔊 15 **Changes**
a real struggle, a sharp rise, adapt, advances, eager, embrace, evolving, fast approaching, let go, major breakthroughs, mind-blowing, new circumstances, unexpected, welcome

🔊 16 **Expressions with *get***
get better, get down to, get information, get into trouble, get more sophisticated, get on somebody's nerves, get out of (the car), get out of (doing something), get over, get ready, get rid of, get to class

2 Project

What changes would you like to see in the future?

TASK: Imagine you have travelled to the future. Give a presentation to the class on the changes you see.

Learning outcomes
1. I can use my creative skills to create an interesting presentation.
2. I can use other people's ideas for inspiration.
3. I can use appropriate language from the unit.

Graphic organiser → Project planner p118

1. 🎥 Watch a video of three students giving their presentation. What aspect of future changes do they describe?

STEP 1: THINK ●●●●

2. Read part of the script and look at the Model slides. Which features do the students include in the first part of their presentation?
   1. attractive presentation slides
   2. the names of the presenters
   3. their chosen changes
   4. a video to illustrate one of the changes
   5. some humour and creativity

STEP 2: PLAN ●●●●

3. Work in pairs. Read the tips in the Super skills box and practise saying the Key phrases with a partner.

CREATIVITY — SUPER SKILLS

Getting inspiration from others

Tips

Try 'blue sky thinking' by getting everyone in the group to share their ideas, even if they sound wild or unsuitable.

Write these ideas on different coloured cards or sticky notes and display them on a poster on the wall.

Look at what the other groups have written for further inspiration. If you decide to copy an idea exactly, remember to ask for permission.

Key phrases

I like/love this idea. What do you think?
Don't you think that this/it is a good/great idea?
Do you mind if we use this idea? We really like it.
Sure! Go ahead! (Scott) came up with that one.

4. Work in groups of three. Brainstorm your ideas for changes in the future onto an A3 poster. Use the tips and Key phrases in the Super skills box.

5. Choose one change for each member of the group. Research your change and make notes.

STEP 3: CREATE ●●●●

6. Read the *How to …* tips on p118 and look at the Model slides. Are they successful? Why/Why not?

7. Create your presentation slides. Use the Model slides, tips and Key phrases to help you.

34   Grammar and Vocabulary → Quick review p33

Model project

WELCOME TO THE FUTURE

We travelled to the future and this is what we saw!

Ash, Scott and Billie

WELCOME TO **THE FUTURE**

- We set our clock to 2050
- Developments in sport
- Amazing advances in mobile technology

Changes in transport

Ash: Hi everyone, it's Ash here and welcome to our presentation all about the future. Our reporters Scott and Billie set the clock for the year 2050. When they got there, they saw some incredible breakthroughs!

Scott: Thanks Ash and welcome to the future, where transport as we know it will be completely unrecognisable! Why? Because they'll have invented teleportation! This means people will be able to travel from anywhere to anywhere in milliseconds. They'll have multiplied the power supply and increased the internet bandwidth to cope with this.

Billie: Yes, I think we can all agree that teleportation will be a huge game changer! Imagine you're at home but there's a big event – say a film premiere in Hollywood – that you really want to go to. In 2050, you'll have time to get ready, be there in time for the film and you won't get into trouble for missing school the next day – because you'll get back before school starts! Isn't that amazing?

Ash: It really is! Thank you Billie and Scott – 2050 sounds incredible. You know, I think I should teleport myself there with the magic of video!

STEP 4: PRESENT

8 Give your presentation to the class and answer any questions.

9 Peer review Listen to the other presentations.
  1. Which presentation did you enjoy the most? Why?
  2. Think of one or two questions to ask each group of time travellers.

2 FINAL REFLECTION

1 The task
Was your presentation organised?
Did you create well-designed slides?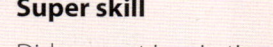

2 Super skill
Did you get inspiration from other students?

3 Language
Did you use new language from this unit? Give examples.

Beyond the task
How could creative skills such as 'blue sky thinking' and/or 'getting inspiration from others' help you to make decisions or solve problems?

3 Perfect

WHAT DOES AN INFLUENCER DO ALL DAY?

WDYT? (What do you think?)

Vocabulary: social media; influencers; word formation: nouns

Grammar: relative clauses; comparing

Reading: an article about fame

Listening: a radio interview about happiness

Speaking: telling an anecdote

Writing: an opinion essay

Project: a video about a perfect day

What's your perfect day?

Follow ▼ **ThisAllyCat**

3,200 likes

ThisAllyCat Beautiful watches at @Ollystime. Use the code 'THISALLYCAT10' to get 10% off. #beautifulwatches

Claire4573 ♡ **@Lydia22sp**

Michelefp98 👍 It's gorgeous! Where can I get one?

Video skills p37

Real-world speaking p43

Project pp46–47

Social media

1 ♻ Match verbs 1–8 with nouns a–h to make phrases connected to social media.

1 change *d*		a	a friend
2 comment		b	an account
3 create		c	a friend request
4 follow		d	your privacy settings
5 (re)set		e	a celebrity
6 send		f	a link
7 share		g	on a post
8 tag		h	your password

2 💬 Work in pairs. Ask and answer questions about the activities in exercise 1. Find at least three things you have in common.

> When was the last time you reset your password?

> I reset my email password last week.

36

Vocabulary 3

My to-dos to boost readership by 50%:

Run a more appealing **blog**
- **Engage** more **with my followers** – **respond to** their **comments**, etc.
- **Review shows, bands** or perhaps even **games**.
- **Launch** at least two new **products** every month.

Attract more YouTube **subscribers**
- **Identify** another **audience**, **create** suitable **content** for them.
- **Subscribe to a** new **channel** and **check out** the **content**.
- **Shoot a** new **video** (get Jollie to edit it – she's amazing!).

Meet up with my **fans**
- **Attend** influencer **event** Tues. @7:00 pm, Park Hotel.
- **Promote** @Ollystime **brand**.

Influencers

3 🎯 Check the meaning of the words in bold in the to-do list. Which of the things in the list can you see in the photos?

4 Complete the text with verbs from the to-do list in the correct form.

1 (…) influencer Iris Apfel's cool looks on social media. She certainly knows how to **2** (…) subscribers – she has almost 1.5 million followers on Instagram. She **3** (…) with her followers and **4** (…) to their comments. She's got considerable experience in **5** (…) new products, **6** (…) brands and **7** (…) important events. As an interior designer, she decorated the White House for nine US presidents! Now as a fashion icon, she skilfully **8** (…) suitable content for her audience.

5 💬 Work in pairs. Complete the sentences with the words in the box. Discuss which ones you agree or disagree with.

> boost readership   create content
> meet up with fans   review more things
> run a blog   shoot a video
> subscribe to their channel

1 It's easy to (…) with your phone if you've got a good camera, but it's much harder to edit it well.
2 I'd rather (…) with weekly posts than (…) for a YouTube channel.
3 If I were a celebrity, I would (…) on a regular basis and allow them to take selfies with me.
4 Many online magazines try to (…) by launching competitions. I think they should (…) so we know what's worth watching, playing or buying.
5 If I like a particular YouTuber, I always (…) .

6 💬 Work in pairs. Answer the questions.
1 Do you follow any influencers? Who? What kinds of things do they promote?
2 Would you like to be an influencer? Why/Why not?
3 If you could run a YouTube channel, what would it be like?

VIDEO SKILLS

7 🎥 Watch the video. What do Oliver's followers all have in common?

8 💬 Work in pairs. Discuss the questions.
1 In your opinion, is this video a typical vlog?
2 Oliver made this video to talk to his followers. In your opinion, is video a good way to do this?

Pronunciation: /b/ and /v/ → p116

3 Reading and critical thinking

An article

1 Read the title of the article. What do you think the article is about?

2 🔊 17 Read and listen to the article. Complete the article with the correct subheadings.
- a From telling jokes to becoming a superstar
- b Using fame to help others
- c Observation skills and hard work

3 Read the article again and answer the questions. Give evidence from the text to support your answers.
1. Why is it easier to get famous now than it was in the past?
2. What event led to Maitane's idea?
3. Why do we get rid of so much good food?
4. What are some of the reasons behind Sartorius' fame?
5. According to the text, what may have contributed to Àngela Màrmol's rise to fame?
6. What is Àngela Màrmol's book about?

4 Are the sentences true or false? Correct the false sentences.
1. Maitane Alonso became famous for organising an international science and technology competition in the USA.
2. Maitane's food preservation idea aims to be safer than current methods.
3. Sartorius made humorous videos before he turned to other types of performance.
4. Sartorius has always created his own content.
5. Like many other TikTokers, Màrmol isn't really into music.
6. The impact of Andy Warhol's work can be seen in the work of other creative people.

5 **Word work** Match the definitions with the words in bold in the article.
1. became known by a lot of people
2. made someone feel worried or upset
3. when food is becoming old and decayed
4. lasting for a brief time
5. something which has come to an end
6. get famous quickly

▶ **Subskill: Understanding the writer's purpose**
To understand a text fully, it's important to understand the writer's purpose. Is the aim to inform, explain, persuade, describe or entertain?

6 Choose the correct option to complete the sentences.
1. The writer describes people as 'ordinary' to make the point that …
   - a most of us will never get famous.
   - b anyone can become famous.
2. The writer talks about the Massachusetts Institute of Technology …
   - a because they're responsible for naming asteroids.
   - b to highlight that Maitane has been noticed by a university.
3. The writer says 'videos up to 15 seconds' and not 'short' to describe the videos on TikTok to …
   - a give the readers more details about TikTok.
   - b emphasise the point about short-lived fame.
4. The writer writes that Àngela Màrmol's videos 'show her actually enjoying music' to suggest that …
   - a other TikTok artists don't like music.
   - b the music is more important than the fame.
5. The writer uses 'game over' in the conclusion …
   - a because Andy Warhol designed video games.
   - b to compare being famous with playing a video game.

7 💬 Work in pairs. Ask and answer the questions.
1. What social media sites do you use? What for?
2. Have you ever received a larger than normal reaction to one of your posts? What happened?
3. Do you think some people count the number of 'likes' on their posts? Should these 'likes' be hidden? Why/Why not?

CRITICAL THINKING

1. **Remember** Which of the people in the article have you heard of?
2. **Analyse** Do you think everyone in the article deserves to be famous? Why?/Why not?
3. **Create** If you were famous, what would you do with your 15 minutes of fame?

FIFTEEN MINUTES OF FAME!

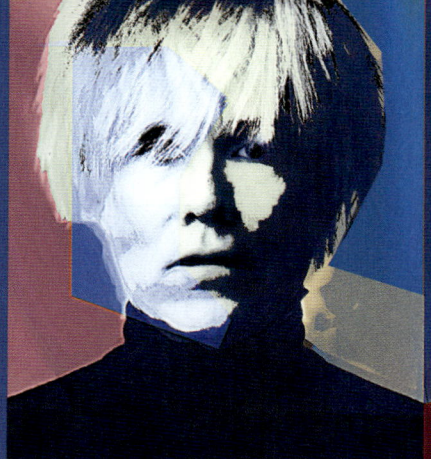

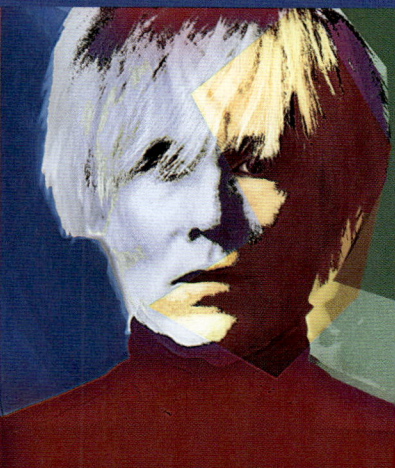

In the late 1960s, Andy Warhol, who was an American artist and filmmaker, predicted that in the future, anyone would be able to rise to fame, even if this fame was **short-lived**. Fast forward to the future and, thanks to the internet and social media sites, there are examples everywhere of ordinary people that have **become an overnight success**.

1 (…)

Maitane Alonso comes from Bilbao, Spain, where she studies medicine at her local university. She rose to media fame after attending an international science and technology competition in Phoenix, USA, and receiving an award. It all started when her father, whose hobby is having barbecues, cooked too much food again. It **bothered** her that people throw away a third of the food we produce because there's no way of keeping it fresh. Maitane invented a new food preservation method that stops food from **going rotten** as quickly in a more sustainable way. It is also a more efficient, faster and cheaper method that aims to reduce the use of chemical substances in food preservation, as they may have harmful effects on our health. As part of her prize, the Massachusetts Institute of Technology will name an asteroid after her. She is now the founder of a company called Innovating Alimentary Machines.

2 (…)

Teenage influencer Jacob Sartorius is an international singer who engages with millions of followers on social media. His journey to success began when he was just eight years old. He turned his passion for making people laugh into online performances. He really **made a name for himself** after lip-syncing videos on Musical.ly, which is now called TikTok, a platform for sharing videos of up to 15 seconds. His next step was to create his own content for his videos and he began to release singles, which are videos or files with one song. Why has Sartorius shot to fame? Of course he's multi-talented, but in addition to that, he's collaborated with other established internet stars, which has boosted his popularity.

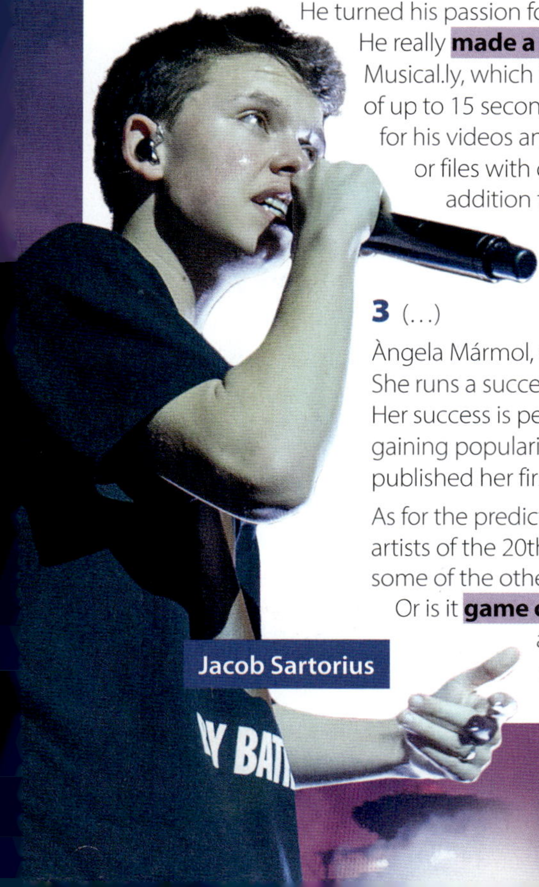

Maitane Alonso

3 (…)

Àngela Mármol, who is a musician and influencer from Barcelona, also has a huge following on TikTok. She runs a successful YouTube channel, too, where she has attracted around 300,000 subscribers. Her success is perhaps due to the fact that her videos show her actually enjoying music. After gaining popularity, Àngela decided to use her celebrity status to raise awareness of bullying and has published her first book about this issue.

As for the prediction we started with, Warhol is still considered to be one of the most influential artists of the 20th century. But did you know some of the other people from this article? Or is it **game over** for them as soon as another internet sensation appears?

Jacob Sartorius

Did you know?
Max the dog got his 15 minutes of fame when he managed to put a car into reverse. He did 'doughnuts', which means driving in circles, for about an hour before the police rescued him. Someone took a video of it and it went viral.

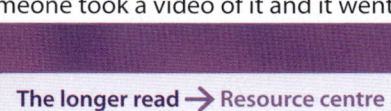

3 Grammar

Relative clauses

1 Read the examples and answer the questions.

> a Andy Warhol, **who** was an American artist and filmmaker, predicted that anyone would be able to rise to fame.
> b There are examples everywhere of ordinary people **that** have become an overnight success.
> c One influencer of **whom** most people have heard is Selena Gomez.

1 Look at the relative clauses in sentences a and b. Which one gives us essential information (defining) and which one gives us extra non-essential information (non-defining)?
2 Do we use commas with defining or non-defining relative clauses?
3 Which relative pronouns do we use for each of these things?
   a people   c possessions   e times
   b things   d places
4 What's the difference between *who* and *whom*?

2 Match 1–5 with a–e to make sentences about social media.

1 There are around 7.8 billion people in the world,
2 There are very few countries in the world
3 More than 90% of us would rather use a brand
4 One of the most important channels for influencer marketing is Instagram,
5 The best time to post on Instagram is 5:00 pm,

a whose users tend to be younger than on Facebook.
b of whom 4.5 billion use the internet.
c when a lot of people engage with the app.
d where there aren't Facebook users.
e which our favourite influencer uses than take advice from an advertiser.

3 Join the phrases to make a question with a relative clause. Use *that* where possible and add commas where necessary.

1 Have you ever posted a video / The video promoted a brand
2 Would you like to live on a tropical island / There's limited internet access
3 Would you use your celebrity status to raise awareness like Àngela Mármol / She uses hers to talk about bullying
4 Do you tag friends on social media / They haven't given you permission
5 Do you remember the day / You first posted something on social media

4 💬 **Work in pairs. Ask and answer the questions in exercise 3.**

5 Choose the correct option to complete the sentences.

> **Omitting the relative pronoun**
> One influencer most people have heard of is Selena Gomez.
> Musical.ly, which TikTok bought in 2017, no longer exists.

1 In the **first**/second example, we have omitted the relative pronoun.
2 The omitted relative pronoun is **which**/**who**.
3 We can omit the relative pronoun when it is the **subject**/**object** of the verb in the relative clause.

6 Complete the article with the correct relative pronouns. If the relative pronoun can be omitted, write '–'.

IT'S ALL A HOAX!

While some people use social media to increase their celebrity status, there are others **1** (…) use it to trick us into believing things **2** (…) are just not true. These are internet hoaxes **3** (…) people say are harmless fun. Lyle Zapato created the 'Pacific Northwest tree octopus', **4** (…) apparently lived in the North American rainforests. He created the content for the Tree Octopus website **5** (…) people could find out more about this curious creature.

Subscribers to Hulu, **6** (…) is an American streaming service, fell for another animal hoax when Hulu announced a 'Hulu Pets' channel **7** (…) animals would enjoy. *The Bark*, **8** (…) is the noise dogs make, was allegedly a programme like *The Voice*, but for dogs.

So, don't forget to double-check your information on a reliable website **9** (…) will confirm what is fact and what is fake.

7 💬 **Work in pairs. Complete the sentences so they are true for you. Compare your sentences with your partner.**

1 I admire celebrities who (…) .
2 I tend to use social media sites which (…) .
3 My favourite time of day is (…) , when (…) .

8 Answer the question to solve the Brain teaser.

BRAIN TEASER

There was a man who was from Greece, who was 15 in 2010 and 10 in 2015.
How is that possible?

Pronunciation: /ʃ/ and /tʃ/ → p116

Vocabulary and Listening 3

Word formation: nouns

1 💬 Work in pairs. What are the people doing in the photos? How do these things bring you happiness?

2 Copy and complete the table with the correct form of the words in the box to make new nouns.

| achieve | equal | happy |
| reader | satisfy | star | young |

-dom	-ity	-ment	-ness	-ship	-th	-tion
boredom						

Word formation: nouns

Understanding suffixes helps boost your vocabulary because you can make so many new words. It is a good idea to write any new words in your notebook. Keep words with a similar ending together. Remember to include any spelling changes, too.

3 Add the correct form of the words in the box to the table in exercise 2. Use a dictionary to help you with the spelling.

~~bored~~	celebrate	champion	creative	enjoy
excite	free	grow	involve	lonely	necessary
participate	relation	relax	strong	warm

4 Complete the dialogues with nouns from exercise 3. Do you agree with them?

A

Working hard is important, but taking time off for **1** *relaxation* is just as necessary.

I agree. I find using my **2** (…), for example by drawing cartoons, really helps to relax.

B

I think **3** (…) in a **4** (…) is much more important than winning or losing it.

You're right, but I think winning boosts your **5** (…).

Yeah, and a close match increases the **6** (…).

5 💬 Work in pairs. Choose four nouns and write a sentence with each one. Compare your ideas. Do you agree with your partner's sentences?

A radio interview

6 🔊 18 Listen to a radio interview with Rebecca Mann. Which of the nouns from exercises 2 and 3 does she mention?

▶ **Subskill: Listening for the information you need**

Read the sentences carefully and think about the kind of information you'll need to listen for, e.g. place, number, name or verb.

7 💬 Work in pairs. Read the sentences. Discuss what kind of information is missing in each one: a verb, a noun or a country?

1 Research shows that teenagers in (…) are happier than most others in the world.
2 Teenagers in this country find it easier to (…) with different people.
3 Teenagers in other countries often have less (…) than these teenagers.
4 They enjoy life and their (…) is high.
5 Students in Los Angeles were in a better mood when they (…) another person.
6 Happiness is part of the school curriculum in (…), (…) and (…).
7 We mustn't forget to celebrate our (…), which can be very small things.
8 Although young people (…) becoming rich and famous, research shows that this does not always bring happiness.

8 Listen again and complete the sentences in exercise 7 with a word or short phrase.

9 💬 Work in groups. Discuss what you and the people you know do to celebrate achievements.

41

3 Grammar

Comparing

1 🗨 Work in pairs. Read the pairs of examples. Do they mean the same thing (S) or something different (D)?

> 1 a Dutch teenagers find it much easier to talk to adults than teens in other countries.
> b Teenagers in other countries don't find it nearly as easy to talk to adults as Dutch teenagers.
> 2 a Dutch teenagers enjoy a bit more freedom than teenagers in other European countries.
> b Dutch teenagers are by far the freest youth group in Europe.

2 Look at the examples in exercise 1 again and complete the rules with *a bit*, *not nearly* or *much*.

1 We use *a lot*, *far* and (…) with comparative adjectives and *by far* with superlative adjectives to describe a big difference.
2 We use *slightly*, *a little* and (…) with comparative adjectives to describe a small difference.
3 We can also use *just*, *not quite* and (…) with *as … as …*

> **as … as, not so/as … as**
>
> We use *as … as* in positive sentences and questions.
> In negative sentences, we can use *so* or *as* with *not*.
> Are young people in other parts of the world as happy as Dutch teenagers?
> Research suggests they aren't as/so happy as Dutch teenagers.

3 Complete the second sentence so that it means the same as the first. Use the words in brackets.

1 It's getting more difficult to find time to see my friends. **(so)**
   It is (…) as before to find time to see my friends.
2 I've never attracted as many followers on social media as now. **(most)**
   These are the (…) attracted.
3 I'm doing fewer subjects at school than last year. **(not)**
   I'm (…) subjects at school as last year.
4 I don't spend nearly as much time on social media as I used to. **(far)**
   I spend (…) on social media than I used to.
5 Not many of my classmates live nearly as far from school as I do. **(lot)**
   I live (…) than most of my classmates.

4 🗨 Work in pairs. Are the sentences in exercise 3 true for you? Why/Why not?

5 Find and correct five mistakes in the questions. One question is correct.

1 Are you just ~~so~~ *as* happy alone as when you're with people?
2 Who's the most funniest person you know?
3 Would you be far lonelier living on a desert island that living in a large city?
4 Is happiness far more desirable than fame and fortune?
5 What's the less interesting TV series you've ever seen?
6 People say winning isn't as important than taking part. Do you agree?

6 🗨 Work in pairs. Ask and answer the questions in exercise 5.

7 Complete the text with one word in each gap.

> **GRAMMAR ROUND-UP**
> 1 2 3 4 5 6 7 8
>
> **THE SECRET TO HAPPINESS?**
> **LOOK AFTER YOUR FRIENDSHIPS!**
>
> Research **1** (…) shown time after time that people **2** (…) enjoy a good relationship with their friends are often **3** (…) happiest. Let's have a brief look at one interesting friendship. **4** (…) you know that singer Rihanna and actress Cara Delevingne have **5** (…) friends **6** (…) over five years? Rihanna and Cara **7** (…) at a fashion show and **8** (…) then, they've known they can count on each other **9** (…) one of them has a problem. Is that the same for you? Can you depend on your friends? **10** (…) you be there the next time your friend needs your help?

> **Research**
>
> Find out more about one or two friendships between famous people. Present your research to your class.

Real-world speaking

Telling an anecdote

1. 🎥 Watch the video. How is Ruth feeling? What happened to her?

2. Watch again. Complete gaps 1–6 in the dialogue.

3. Watch again. Which Key phrases do you hear?

Ruth: Guess who I've just seen!

Simon: Who? Was it someone famous?

Ruth: Yeah! It was the 1 (…) from that new TV show.

Simon: I don't know who you mean.

Ruth: You know! He was a professional 2 (…) who played in the Premier League until he got injured!

Simon: Yeah, but who is he? What is he known for now?

Ruth: Now he's the 3 (…) on that new reality show which 4 (…) is talking about at the moment.

Simon: Cool! Where did you see him?

Ruth: I was out with a 5 (…) when we saw him. He was standing next to that clock in town where we usually meet up. He was just 6 (…) there. I couldn't believe it!

Simon: Did you get a selfie?

Ruth: Of course I did! Do you want to see it?

4. Create your own dialogue. Follow the steps in the Skills boost.

SKILLS BOOST

THINK
You've just met someone famous. Make notes about it.

PREPARE
Prepare a dialogue. Remember to include relative clauses to describe the experience and Key phrases to show interest.

PRACTISE
Practise your dialogue.

PERFORM
Act out your dialogue for the class.

5. **Peer review** Listen to your classmates and answer the questions.
   1. Did they describe the experience well?
   2. Which Key phrases did they use?

Key phrases

Describing what happened
Guess who I've just seen!
Before you ask, he/she/it was …
He/She/It is/was a … who … / Now he/she …
I was out with … when …
He/She was … (having lunch).
I couldn't believe it! / It was unbelievable!

Showing interest
Who?/Who's that? / Yeah, but who is he/she?
Where did you see him/her?
Who was he/she with? / What was he/she doing?
Cool!/Wow!/Amazing!
Did you get a selfie?

Real-world grammar

I don't know *who* you mean.

Phrasebook → p123

3 Writing

Some people think that celebrities deserve more privacy than they have. Do you agree?

(1) Open up any web page, magazine or newspaper and you can find photos, news and gossip about famous people. Where does the press get this information from? Some journalists follow celebrities everywhere they go and no doubt invade their private lives. **My personal view** is that famous people deserve more privacy than this.

(2) **To begin with**, many sportspeople, actors or musicians become famous because of their jobs. Surely they also have the right to a day off alone with their friends or family?

(3) **Secondly, I personally feel** that we should remember these people for what they do, for example, for being an amazing performer, rather than for what they wear to do their shopping or what they look like on a Sunday morning.

(4) **Finally**, celebrities have feelings and emotions like us. Being surrounded by the press or chased down the street must be quite terrifying and is probably quite dangerous. They should be allowed to walk around freely without being bothered.

(5) **In conclusion**, although some people might argue that fame comes with a price, **I firmly believe** that everyone has the right to a private life. **I would go further to say** that some journalists go to extremes to get their perfect story and we should do more to stop this.

An opinion essay

1 Read the title of the essay. What's your own opinion on the question?

2 Read the essay. Does the writer agree or disagree with the statement? Do they give one or both sides of the argument?

3 Match descriptions a–d with paragraphs 1–5. Which description is used more than once? Which one is not used? Why?

   a   give an argument for and support it
   b   give an argument against and support it
   c   conclude by stating your opinion again
   d   introduce the topic and state your opinion

▶ **Subskill: Organising your essay**

Organise your essay into four or five paragraphs: an introduction, two or three arguments in separate paragraphs and a conclusion. Use words like *Firstly, Secondly, Finally* and *In conclusion* at the beginning of each paragraph to help the reader follow your argument.

4 Read the information on organising your essay. Copy and complete the table with the expressions in bold in the essay.

State an opinion	In my opinion
Introduce an argument	Firstly
Extend the argument	What's more, I'd like to add
Conclude	To sum up

44

5 Read the essay question. Then order the paragraph beginnings to make an essay plan.

> Some people think that it's unfair that celebrities earn much more than people in other important professions, like nurses or teachers. What do you think?

a Secondly, many celebrities do not do much more than …

b Finally, everyone deserves the right to …

c To sum up, although some people would argue that we need celebrities, I firmly believe …

d Open up any gossip magazine and you can find stories about celebrities and their expensive lifestyles or their shopping sprees. But is this fair when others earn much less? I personally feel …

e Firstly, people in professions such as nursing or teaching have studied …

6 Follow the steps in the Skills boost to answer the essay question in exercise 5.

SKILLS BOOST

THINK
Read the question carefully and decide if you agree or disagree. Think of three different arguments to support your opinion and make notes.

PREPARE
Organise your notes into five sections. Use the Subskill to help you.

WRITE
Write your opinion essay. Use your notes to help you.

CHECK
Read your essay. Answer the questions.
1 Have you organised your essay into logical paragraphs?
2 Have you used the expressions in exercise 4 to develop your argument?
3 Have you used some of the grammar and vocabulary from the unit?

7 **Peer review** Exchange your opinion essay with another student. Answer the questions.
1 Has the writer organised their essay into clear paragraphs?
2 Does the writer state their opinion and give at least three reasons to support it?
3 Do they reach a conclusion and then open up the argument further?

QUICK REVIEW 3

Grammar

Relative clauses
With **defining relative clauses**, we don't use commas, and we can replace *who* or *which* with *that*. We can omit the relative pronoun if it's the object of the clause.
*There are examples everywhere of ordinary people **that have become an overnight success**.*
*The app **(which/that) I downloaded yesterday** is great for editing videos.*
With **non-defining relative clauses**, we use commas, and we can't replace *who* or *which* with *that*. We can't omit the relative pronoun.
*Musical.ly, **which TikTok bought in 2017**, no longer exists.*

Comparing
We use *a lot*, *far* and *much* with comparative adjectives and *by far* with superlative adjectives to describe a big difference.
We use *slightly*, *a little* and *a bit* with comparative adjectives to describe a small difference.
*Dutch teenagers find it **much easier** to talk to adults **than** teens in other countries.*
*Dutch teenagers are **by far the freest** young people in Europe.*
*Dutch teenagers enjoy **a bit more freedom than** teenagers in other European countries.*

as … as, not so/as … as
We can also use *just*, *not quite* and *not nearly* with *as … as …*
*Are young people in other parts of the world **as** happy **as** Dutch teenagers?*
*Teenagers in other countries do**n't** find it **nearly as/so easy** to talk to their parents **as** Dutch teenagers.*

Vocabulary

🔊 19 **Social media**
change your privacy settings, comment on a post, create an account, follow a celebrity, reset your password, send a friend request, set your password, share a link, tag a friend

🔊 20 **Influencers**
attend an event, attract subscribers, boost readership, check out content, create content, engage with followers, identify an audience, launch products, meet up with fans, promote a brand, respond to comments, review shows, bands or games, run a blog, shoot a video, subscribe to a channel

🔊 21 **Word formation: nouns**
achievement, boredom, celebration, championship, creativity, enjoyment, equality, excitement, freedom, growth, happiness, involvement, loneliness, necessity, participation, readership, relationship, relaxation, satisfaction, stardom, strength, warmth, youth

3 Project

WDYT? (What do you think?)
What's your perfect day?

TASK: Create a 'What's your perfect day?' video for a class YouTube channel.

Learning outcomes
1 I can create interesting content and engage my audience with a video.
2 I can use appropriate grammar and vocabulary from the unit in my video.
3 I can use collaboration skills to work effectively in a small group.

Graphic organiser → Project planner p119

1 🎥 Watch part of a video called 'Our Perfect Day'. What activity would Billie and Scott do together?

STEP 1: THINK

2 Look at the timeline in the Model project. What do we use this for?

3 Think about the script for the video. Which of these things will you need to include?
- a location
- b actors
- c music
- d props
- e actions
- f the timing
- g what each person says

STEP 2: PLAN

4 Work in pairs. Read the tips in the Super skills box and practise saying the Key phrases with a partner.

COLLABORATION — SUPER SKILLS

Successfully completing the task as a team

Tips
Agree on a time frame.
Spend time brainstorming ideas together; listen to each other and propose alternative approaches.
Divide up the work fairly and check that everyone is sticking to the established schedule.

Key phrases
We'll need to have uploaded the video by … , so when do we need to have … by?
That's an interesting idea, but do you think it'll engage our audience/attract more views?
Shall we try to come up with some alternatives?
Who wants to work on … ?
Is everyone happy with what they're doing?
Does anyone feel they got more/less than the others?
Do you need a hand with anything?

5 Work in groups of three. Agree on a time frame and draw a timeline. Use the tips and Key phrases in the Super skills box.

6 Brainstorm ideas for each part of your perfect day. Then decide who will create the content for each part and make notes.

STEP 3: CREATE

7 Read the *How to …* tips on p119. Write the script for your video using the Model project. Then film your video.

8 Choose the best parts of the video and edit it. Add music to make it more interesting.

Model project

OUR PERFECT DAY

TODAY = FRIDAY 5TH
- Decide on time frame
- Brainstorm ideas
- Divide up work

WEEKEND
- Research information

TUESDAY 9TH
- Work on video scripts

FRIDAY 12TH
- Combine video scripts
- Decide on location, music, props, etc.

WEEKEND
- Shoot and edit video
- Add in music
- Pre-screening

TUESDAY 16TH
- Video screening in class
- Reflect on work

STEP 4: PRESENT

9 Upload your video to a host site or show it to the class. Be prepared to answer any questions.

10 **Peer review** Watch the other videos and answer the questions. If the videos are online, use the *like* button and leave a comment.
  1. Which video was the most engaging? Why?
  2. Think of a question to ask your classmates about how they decided to put the video together.
  3. Think of something you like about each video.

3 FINAL REFLECTION

1. **The task**
   Did you manage to engage your viewers in your video?

2. **Super skill**
   Did you collaborate effectively as a group?
   Did you meet the deadline?

3. **Language**
   Did you use new language from this unit? Give examples.

Beyond the task
Would an 'Ideas for a Perfect Day' channel be successful among young people? What would make young people interested in it? Think about the presenter, style and tone, content, music, etc.

47

4 Natural world

WDYT? (What do you think?)
What is the best way to enjoy nature?

Vocabulary: places; natural world; words that are nouns and verbs

Grammar: modal verbs; perfect modals

Reading: a travel guide about the Seven Natural Wonders of the World

Listening: a podcast about natural disaster films

Speaking: giving instructions

Writing: a description of a place

Project: a video proposal for a Natural Wonder of the World

Video skills p49

Real-world speaking p55

Project pp58–59

ARE YOU A SURVIVOR?

1. You're skiing in the mountains when there's an **avalanche**. You …
   a start skiing away.
   b find a big rock or tree to hold on to.

2. There's a **volcanic eruption** when you're visiting a nearby city. You …
   a carry on looking around.
   b get out of there as fast as you can.

3. You're hiking through a **canyon** when there's a **tornado** and heavy rain. There's going to be a **flash flood**. You …
   a hide in a **cave** and scream for help.
   b find a high place to climb up.

Places

1 Look at the words in the box. Can you add any more to the list? Answer the questions.

| beach | coast | desert | forest | hill | jungle |
| lake | mountain | ocean | river | volcano |

Which … ?
1 are water
2 are found near water
3 are high places
4 is a very dry place
5 have lots of trees together

2 Work in pairs. Ask and answer the questions.
1 When was the last time you went to each of these places? What did you do there?
2 Which of these places do you like most/least? Why?

I went to the beach last summer. We …

My favourite place is the mountains because …

Vocabulary 4

4 You're exploring a **harbour** on an island. You think you see a **tsunami**, so you …
  a swim out to the **coral reef** and hide there.
  b climb the nearest hill – fast!

5 You're in a boat on a river when you come to a small **cliff** with a **waterfall**. You …
  a decide to stay in the boat.
  b go to the **riverbank** to evaluate what to do next.

6 There's a **drought** after a **heatwave** and you're out walking in the countryside when you see a **wildfire** in the distance. You …
  a continue walking in the area.
  b look for the **shore** of a nearby lake and get in the water.

7 You're at home during an **earthquake**. You …
  a run outside to get safe.
  b hide under a heavy table.

8 If there was a **landslide**, you would …
  a go outside to see the damage.
  b leave quickly and avoid rivers and **valleys**.

Mostly 'a's: You should brush up on your survival skills!
Mostly 'b's: Congratulations! You could survive anything!

Natural world

3 Read the quiz and check the meaning of the words in bold.

4 Work in pairs. Do the quiz. Who is more likely to survive?

5 Copy and complete the table with the words in bold from the quiz.

Geographical features	Natural disasters
canyon	avalanche

6 Complete the sentences with words in bold from the quiz.
  1 During a (…) , there is very little or no rain, which means there isn't much water to drink.
  2 A (…) is a very large wave which is caused by an earthquake.
  3 An (…) is a sudden shaking of the ground.
  4 In an (…) , snow moves very fast down a mountain.
  5 A (…) is when water from a river or the rain covers places suddenly and unexpectedly.
  6 A (…) starts in the countryside and can spread quickly and in an uncontrolled way.
  7 A (…) is an extremely strong wind that spins round.
  8 During a (…) , a large amount of earth and rocks falls down the side of a mountain or steep slope.

7 Write definitions for the geographical features in exercise 5.

8 Work in pairs. Ask and answer the questions.
  1 Which geographical features in exercise 5 have you visited? When? What were they like?
  2 Which natural disasters are most/least likely to happen in summer/winter? Which are not seasonal?

VIDEO SKILLS

9 Watch the video. What geographical features do you see?

10 Work in pairs. Discuss the questions.
  1 This video uses a lot of aerial shots. Why do you think this is?
  2 Do you think Steve makes these vlogs alone? Why/Why not?

4 Reading and critical thinking

A travel guide

1 Look at the photos on p51. For each one, what related vocabulary do you remember?

2 What do you know about 1–7? Where are they? Can you match each one to a photo?
1. the Grand Canyon
2. the Great Barrier Reef
3. the northern lights
4. the harbour of Rio de Janeiro
5. Mount Everest
6. Paricutín
7. Victoria Falls

3 🔊 22 Read the guide quickly. Complete 1–7 in the guide with the places in exercise 2. Then listen and check your answers.

▶ **Subskill: Identifying fact and opinion**
Facts can be proved to be true. Opinions are things people think or believe, so they are neither correct nor incorrect.

4 Read the guide again. Are sentences 1–8 facts (F) or opinions (O)?
1. The northern lights are caused by solar particles.
2. Paricutín appeared in an eruption in 1943.
3. Paricutín deserves to be one of the Seven Natural Wonders of the World.
4. The harbour in Rio de Janeiro is a beautiful place to explore.
5. You can see the spray from the Victoria Falls from far away in the wet season.
6. The best time to see the Victoria Falls is at full moon.
7. Mount Everest is the most famous natural wonder.
8. Diving in the Great Barrier Reef is the most incredible experience you'll ever have.

5 Are the sentences true or false? Correct the false sentences.
1. The northern lights are always visible.
2. Paricutín is almost 422 m taller now than when it first appeared.
3. You can hike along all of the Grand Canyon.
4. The Victoria Falls is by far the biggest waterfall in the world.
5. The Great Barrier Reef is one huge coral reef that covers 344,000 km².

6 Answer the questions.
1. In what two ways are the northern lights different from the other wonders?
2. Why is Paricutín so special?
3. What three different ways to see the Grand Canyon does the writer mention?
4. What has helped make the harbour at Rio popular?
5. What makes the Victoria Falls worth visiting?
6. When was Everest climbed for the first time?
7. What two things make the Great Barrier Reef so special?

7 **Word work** Match the definitions with the words in bold in the guide.
1. travel on a small light boat, usually made of plastic
2. a place to visit that is very popular with visitors
3. an occasion when a lot of people are asked about an issue to assess how popular something is
4. extremely impressive
5. a list of things you want to do in your lifetime
6. the situation when an animal or plant no longer exists, or a volcano is no longer active
7. many drops of water forced into the air together

8 💬 Work in pairs. Answer the questions.
1. Which of the Seven Natural Wonders would you most like to visit/see? Why?
2. How do you think we should look after these places?

CRITICAL THINKING
1. **Understand** Explain what makes each wonder special.
2. **Analyse** Compare the wonders and put them in order from most to least interesting, in your opinion.
3. **Evaluate** Justify your choices, giving reasons for them.

Research
Rio de Janeiro means 'River of January'. It was given its name by a Portuguese explorer who arrived there in January and thought the harbour was the mouth of a river.

Find out which of the other Natural Wonders have a local name and how Mount Everest, Victoria Falls and the northern lights got their names.

THE 7 WONDERS

Did you know?
The Great Barrier Reef is the only living thing you can see from space.

The Seven Natural Wonders of the World were chosen in a global **popularity poll** and with so many amazing options to choose from, it can't have been easy to decide which places to vote for. All these incredible sights are definitely on our **bucket list**, so we had to write about them.

1 (…) are unusual because you can see them from different places and they're in the sky rather than on land. They're actually there all the time, but you can't see them unless the conditions are right. Then amazing lights appear to move across the sky, constantly changing. In the past, people thought they could be magic, but scientists now know they're caused by solar particles.

You might not have heard of **2** (…) in Mexico, but it's the only volcano that humans have ever seen form. Now almost 424 m high, it started as a two-metre high volcano that appeared during an eruption in 1943. It's been inactive since 1952, so geologists were able to study it from creation to **extinction**. Although it's not beautiful, we believe it deserves a place on the list.

At over 400 km long, **3** (…) in the USA is one of the biggest wonders and you can hike or **raft** along parts of it. There are strict laws to protect wildlife, so you mustn't feed any animals and you should watch out for snakes. Going on a helicopter tour here is definitely a luxury worth paying for, we think.

With over 100 islands and stretching over 30 km, **4** (…) in Brazil is a beautiful place to explore. You don't have to go on a boat trip to enjoy it – you can climb to the top of Corcovado for **spectacular** views. The 40-m high statue of Christ the Redeemer there has helped make this wonder a top **tourist attraction**.

5 (…), on the border of Zambia and Zimbabwe, is one of the largest waterfalls in the world – that alone makes it worth a visit. It's 1.7 km wide and 108 m high. During the wet season, you can see the powerful **spray** from 50 km away! The best time to see it is probably during a full moon when a night-time rainbow forms, creating an unforgettable sight.

At over 8,848 m high, **6** (…) is perhaps the most famous natural wonder. Located between Nepal and Tibet, it's the highest mountain in the world and climbers weren't able to reach the top until 1953. To climb it, you have to be extremely fit. Luckily, there are great views of this giant from a distance, which in our opinion is the best way to enjoy it.

7 (…) covers about 344,000 km^2 and is home to many species of marine life – its size and the fact that it has over 1,500 species of fish, around 400 types of coral and 240 bird species make it totally unique. Diving in one of the 3,000 coral reefs there is perhaps one of the most incredible experiences you'll ever have.

→ Visit our website and book your next holiday now. Click the links to see our recommendations for places to stay and other useful information.

The longer read → Resource centre

4 Grammar

Modal verbs

1 Read the examples and answer the questions.

Present	Past
Ability	
You can/can't hike along the canyon.	We were able to pay for a helicopter tour. We couldn't/weren't able to pay for a helicopter tour.
Obligation and prohibition	
You must/have to keep to the paths in the park. You mustn't feed the animals. It's illegal. You don't have to/don't need to go today.	We had to write about our holiday. They weren't allowed to feed the animals. We didn't have to/didn't need to pay – it was free.
Possibility, deduction and certainty	
It can't be easy to climb Everest. Helicopter rides must be expensive. They think Luke might/could/may be lost in the canyon.	It can't/couldn't have been easy to decide. It must have been amazing to see. You may/might/could have been too far away to see the mist.

1. When do we have to use *was/were able to* instead of *could*?
2. Is there a past form of *must/mustn't* and *may/might*?
3. Which verbs do we use to talk about possibility and certainty in the past?

2 Choose the correct answers to complete the sentences.

1. You **mustn't/don't have to/have to** canoe down the river. It isn't permitted.
2. People **don't have to/mustn't/can't** visit the museum in the morning. It's open in the afternoon, too.
3. We thought the tour would be full, but in the end we **could/were able to/mustn't** get tickets.
4. They **mustn't/couldn't/didn't have to** walk home alone; they had to walk together.
5. You **can/must/have to** walk along the shore if you like.

should
We use *should* in the present to give advice and make recommendations.
You should visit Rio – it's amazing.
You shouldn't go hiking without telling anyone.

3 Complete the sentences with the correct form of a suitable modal verb. There may be more than one possible answer.

1. There are lots of walks you (…) do in the area, but you (…) leave the main paths. That's our advice.
2. There are bears in the area, so you (…) leave food in your tent; it's too dangerous. You (…) tell the park ranger if you see a bear – that's a rule.
3. We (…) build a shop near the park entrance last year – finally. We (…) do it, but we wanted to improve the camp!
4. Last year, people (…) use the lake path because it wasn't clear. We cleared it two months ago so people (…) enjoy walking by the lake.

4 Rewrite the sentences with modal verbs of speculation and deduction. Use the words in bold to help you.

1. **It's possible** that Magda explored the canyon.
2. **There's no way** that they are in Brazil now. I'm **sure** they are at home.
3. **The only possibility** is that they rafted down the river. It is **not possible** that they walked.
4. **Maybe** they are lost. **It's possible** that they left the path.
5. **It's extremely unlikely** that they saw a bear.

5 Complete the text with the correct form of a modal verb and the verbs in brackets. There may be more than one possible answer.

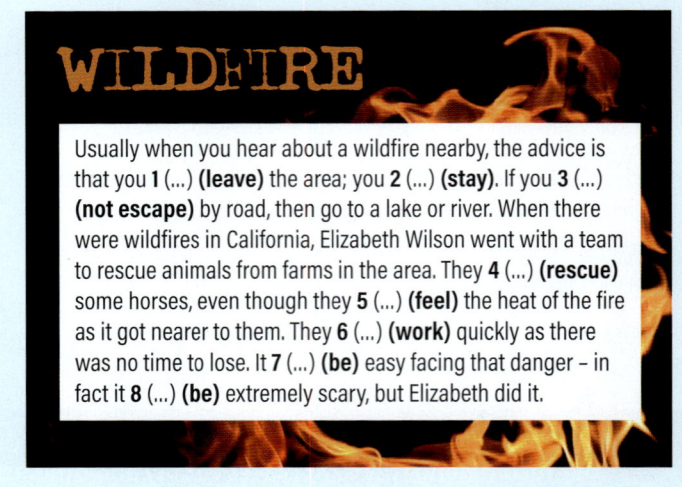

WILDFIRE

Usually when you hear about a wildfire nearby, the advice is that you **1** (…) **(leave)** the area; you **2** (…) **(stay)**. If you **3** (…) **(not escape)** by road, then go to a lake or river. When there were wildfires in California, Elizabeth Wilson went with a team to rescue animals from farms in the area. They **4** (…) **(rescue)** some horses, even though they **5** (…) **(feel)** the heat of the fire as it got nearer to them. They **6** (…) **(work)** quickly as there was no time to lose. It **7** (…) **(be)** easy facing that danger – in fact it **8** (…) **(be)** extremely scary, but Elizabeth did it.

6 Answer the question to solve the Brain teaser.

BRAIN TEASER
Sam spent two days in hospital. When he left, he had to be carried out of the hospital; he couldn't walk out.

Why was he in hospital?

Words that are nouns and verbs

1 Look at the words in the box. Answer the questions.

> aim break challenge change decrease
> demand film help impact increase name
> object permit progress rescue research
> surprise suspect

1 What is the meaning of the noun form and verb form of each word?
2 Do you know any other words like this?

2 Read the article. Are the words in bold nouns or verbs?

Why do we love natural disaster films?

From floods to ice ages, avalanches to forest fires … you **name** it, there's been a **film** about it. Surprisingly, there's been an **increase** not a **decrease** in natural disaster films over recent years, and I **suspect** this trend isn't going to **change**. It's no **surprise** that people enjoy adventure stories, but why is **demand** for disaster so high?

Changing word stress

Some two-syllable words that are both nouns and verbs can have different word stress. The noun is stressed on the first syllable and the verb is stressed on the second syllable.

3 🔊 23 Complete the sentences with the correct form of the words in brackets. Which ones have a different word stress? Listen and check.

1 Humans have (…) **(progress)** a lot in the past century, but the (…) **(impact)** on the planet has been huge.
2 If there was a disaster, I'd try to (…) **(rescue)** people if I could. I'd like to be a (…) **(rescue)** worker.
3 There's been a (…) **(decrease)** in the use of technology among young people.
4 It would (…) **(surprise)** me if the popularity of disaster films (…) **(decrease)**.
5 I'm making great (…) **(progress)** with learning English. It isn't so (…) **(challenge)** this year.
6 The last film I saw really (…) **(impact)** on me.
7 For me, it's a (…) **(challenge)** to learn new vocabulary.
8 Teachers shouldn't give students (…) **(surprise)** tests.

Vocabulary and Listening 4

4 💬 Work in pairs. Do you agree with the sentences in exercise 3? Why/Why not?

A podcast

▶ **Subskill: Using prior knowledge**
Thinking about and discussing what you already know about a topic prepares you to listen.
Be careful when you answer questions: only use the information in the listening, not your own ideas.

5 Think about the three points and use them to answer questions 1–5.
- what you know from exercise 2
- your own experience
- your own knowledge

1 How long have films about disasters been around?
2 Do films about natural disasters make a lot of money?
3 Who do viewers usually care about? The main characters? Everyone? Only the survivors?
4 What qualities do the main characters usually show? Are they perfect?
5 When real life is hard, do people enjoy this type of film more or less? Why?

6 🔊 24 Listen to the podcast and check your answers in exercise 5.

7 Listen again. Complete the sentences with between one and three words or a number.
1 The first disaster film, *Fire*, was made in (…) .
2 The film *Deluge* was about a (…) which affected the city of (…) .
3 Worldwide, the film *Geostorm* made almost $(…) .
4 Disaster films make us think it is possible to (…) .
5 The (…) that the presenter watched terrified her.

8 💬 Work in pairs. Do you enjoy films about natural disasters? What do you like/dislike about them? Give reasons for your answers.

Pronunciation: Word stress: nouns and verbs → p117

4 Grammar

Perfect modals

1 Read the examples and match sentences 1–6 with explanations a–f.

> 1 I could have told you that, but I didn't.
> 2 I couldn't have done that, even if I had wanted to.
> 3 I should have trained as a film producer.
> 4 I shouldn't have watched the film.
> 5 I would have watched a disaster film, but there wasn't one on.
> 6 The film was scary. I wouldn't have watched it normally.

a I didn't do this and I now wish I had done it.
b I didn't do it. It was impossible for me or I didn't know about it. (If I had known or been able to, I would have done it.)
c I didn't do this, but it was possible for me to do it.
d I did this and now I wish I hadn't done it. I regret it.
e I did this, but I would have acted differently in other circumstances or if I'd known more.
f I didn't do this. It was impossible for me to do it.

2 Complete the sentences with the perfect form of the modal verbs in brackets.

1 It was the wrong thing to do. I (…) **(should not / do)** it.
2 Why didn't you tell me you didn't understand the homework? I (…) **(would / help)** you.
3 I was late because the bus didn't come, so I ran all the way. I (…) **(could not / arrive)** any earlier.
4 I bought a new jacket instead of repairing my old one. I suppose I (…) **(could / mend)** it instead.
5 I'm so tired today. I (…) **(should / go)** to bed earlier.

3 💬 Work in pairs. Correct the sentences. One sentence is correct. Then compare in pairs. Which sentences are true for you?

1 I could gone out last night, but I didn't.
2 Last week, I did something I shouldn't have did – I wish I hadn't!
3 I would have done my homework last night, but I'd forgotten my books.
4 The last time someone gave me a message for my friend, I forgot about it. I have told my friend, but I didn't.
5 We had so much homework yesterday that I could have finished it even if I'd worked all night.

4 Complete the sentences with a perfect modal verb and the correct form of the verbs in brackets.

1 It's a pity you missed the film – you (…) **(love)** it!
2 Even if I'd studied more, I (…) **(pass)** the exam – it was impossibly hard. Nobody passed.
3 Why did you lie? You (…) **(tell)** me the truth!
4 They didn't try hard enough. They're really good swimmers and they (…) **(win)** the competition.

5 Complete the sentences with perfect modal verbs. Use your own ideas.

1 I didn't (…) I would (…).
2 Yesterday, I should (…).
3 This morning, I shouldn't (…).
4 Last weekend, I could (…).
5 I didn't (…) I couldn't (…).

6 Choose the correct option to complete the text.

GRAMMAR ROUND-UP
1 2 3 4 **5 6 7 8**

AN AMAZING HIKE

1 Had you been/Have you been/Were you doing long hikes for several years now? Do you want an exciting challenge? The new Route of Parks **2 can't/could/must** be for you. It's a new trail **3 where/which/whose** goes from Puerto Montt to Cape Horn and is nearly 2,800 km long. Although it's **4 a bit/by far/not nearly** as long as the Pacific Crest Trail (almost 4,300 km), it joins 17 national parks together, so the scenery is amazing. By the end of the trail, you **5 will be seeing/will have seen/will see** some incredible things, including the Andes Mountains, rainforests and several volcanoes. It **6 can't/might/must** have been easy to create this amazing route and it **7 mustn't/shouldn't/wouldn't** have been possible without the Conservation Land Trust. This foundation was created by Kristine and Douglas Tompkins, who **8 bought/had been buying/have been buying** millions of acres of land in Chile during the 1990s to protect it and then gave it to the Chilean government in 2017.

Research

Find out more about the Route of Parks, the Appalachian Trail or the Pacific Crest Trail.

Real-world speaking 4

Giving instructions

1 🎥 Watch the video. Where does Jason advise Gabby to put her valuables?

2 Watch again. Complete gaps 1–6 in the dialogue.

Gabby: I'm really stuck with my packing.

Jason: You should have packed yesterday!

Gabby: I know, but I couldn't do it then. Now I've got far too much.

Jason: First, put your **1** (…) in two piles. What do you definitely need? What can you leave behind? And make sure you roll the clothes up so they take up less space.

Gabby: Yes, and now I can fit in some more clothes!

Jason: Try not to fill your case – then there's space for your holiday **2** (…).

Gabby: Oh, right. Well, I'll just put my tablet, passport and plane ticket in the case.

Jason: Whatever you do, don't put **3** (…) in your case! Put them in your hand **4** (…).

Gabby: OK. Now, have I forgotten anything?

Jason: Remember the **5** (…) for all your digital devices and check whether you need an **6** (…)! Always pack them in a small bag so they'll be easy to find.

Gabby: Done! Thanks so much for your help!

3 Read the Key phrases. Which ones are in the dialogue?

4 Create your own dialogue. Follow the steps in the Skills boost.

SKILLS BOOST

THINK
Choose one of the types of bags below and think of tips for packing it. Make notes.
- backpack   • school bag   • lunch bag

PREPARE
Prepare your dialogue. Remember to use the Key phrases for giving instructions and modal verbs.

PRACTISE
Practise your dialogue.

PERFORM
Act out your dialogue for the class.

5 Peer review Listen to your classmates. Answer the questions.
1. How many tips for packing do they give?
2. Which Key phrases do they use?

Key phrases
Make sure you/Be sure to …
Whatever you do, don't …
Don't forget (to)/Remember (to) …
Under no circumstances should you …
It's important to/It helps to/You need to …
Try (not) to …
Always/Never …

Real-world grammar
You **should have packed** yesterday!
What **can** you leave behind?

Phrasebook → p123

55

4 Writing

Isla Mujeres Places to go · Things to do · Plan your trip

A You might not have heard of Isla Mujeres, but if you're lucky enough to visit Mexico, it's somewhere you should consider staying. This small and friendly island is one of my favourite parts of the country and it's only 13 km from Cancún. There's an excellent range of places to stay, great facilities and plenty of activities to make the trip **worthwhile**.

B The coast is **picturesque**: there are kilometres of beautiful **unspoilt** beaches and incredible coral reefs, which are perfect for snorkelling. The island is well known for its wildlife – you can go diving with dolphins or whale sharks, visit the turtle sanctuary or go bird-watching on a nearby island. If you prefer, you can simply relax on the white sandy beaches and swim in the clear warm water. If you're feeling **adventurous**, why not explore the island by golf cart and visit the ancient Mayan temple ruins and the lighthouse? The main town is a **charming** place, too. You'll find plenty of shops filled with traditional local crafts, jewellery and clothes. In the evening, try some **mouth-watering** fresh dishes at one of the restaurants.

C Although I'd especially recommend Isla Mujeres to water sports fans and as a place to relax, the island has something for everyone. Whatever your reason for coming, you're sure to enjoy it.

A description of a place

1 Read the text and answer the questions.
1. Where would you find this kind of text?
2. Does the writer like Isla Mujeres? How do you know?

2 Read the text again. In which paragraph (A–C) does the writer …
1. talk about places of interest and things to do?
2. recommend visiting the place?
3. say where the place is?

3 Match definitions 1–6 with the adjectives in bold in the text.
1. keen to try new or exciting things
2. very attractive and pleasant
3. which tastes or smells extremely nice
4. worth the time, money or effort
5. beautiful and scenic (place or landscape)
6. beautiful because it has not been changed or damaged

▶ Subskill: Using articles correctly

It is very important to know when to use the indefinite article (*a/an*) or definite article (*the*), and when to use no article.

4 Complete the rules with *the*, *a/an* or no article (–).
1. We use (…) before singular countable nouns, the first time something is mentioned and in some expressions of quantity.
2. We use (…) with singular and plural and countable and uncountable nouns when we refer to something already mentioned or have a specific thing in mind.
3. We use (…) before cities, place names and languages, and when we are talking about people or things in general.

5 Complete the text with *the*, *a/an* or no article (–). Use the rules in exercise 4 to help you.

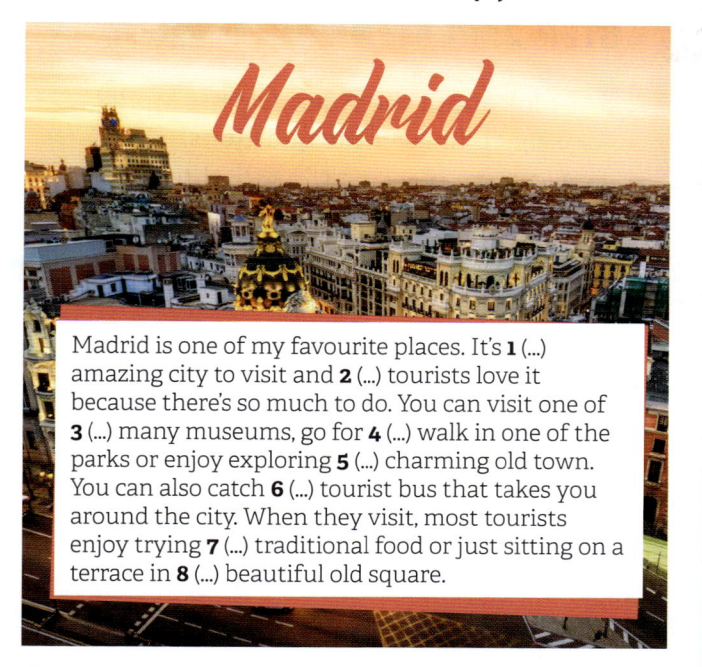

Madrid

Madrid is one of my favourite places. It's **1** (...) amazing city to visit and **2** (...) tourists love it because there's so much to do. You can visit one of **3** (...) many museums, go for **4** (...) walk in one of the parks or enjoy exploring **5** (...) charming old town. You can also catch **6** (...) tourist bus that takes you around the city. When they visit, most tourists enjoy trying **7** (...) traditional food or just sitting on a terrace in **8** (...) beautiful old square.

6 Write a description of a place. Follow the steps in the Skills boost.

SKILLS BOOST

THINK
Decide which place to write about. Look at the paragraph descriptions in exercise 2: do you need to research any information for the paragraphs? Find the information you need and make notes.

PREPARE
Organise your notes into three paragraphs. Use the paragraph plan in exercise 2 to help you.

WRITE
Write your description. Use the model and your notes to help you.

CHECK
Read your description and answer the questions.
1 Have you used articles correctly?
2 Have you used modal verbs?
3 Have you included vocabulary from the unit?
4 Have you used descriptive adjectives effectively?

7 **Peer review** Exchange your description with another student. Answer the questions.
1 Read your partner's description. Have they organised it well?
2 Has your partner included all the things in the checklist?
3 Would you like to visit this place? Why/Why not?

QUICK REVIEW 4

Grammar

Modal verbs
We use modal verbs to talk about possibility, obligation/no obligation and for deduction and speculation.

Present
You **can/can't** hike along the lake shore.
Hurry! We **may/might** miss the bus to the harbour.
You **must/have to** stay on the paths.
People **mustn't** feed the animals there.
You **don't have/need to** go if you don't want to.
That **must** be a new volcano – it wasn't there before.
It **can't** be a deep lake; I can see the bottom.
I suppose it **might/could/may** be dangerous. I don't know.
You **should/shouldn't** go to the island. That's my advice.

Past
We **could/couldn't** canoe on the lake.
They **were/weren't able to** reach the mountain top.
We **had to** go with a guide; it was obligatory.
I **didn't have/need to** pay. It was free.
It **must have** been amazing to see the volcano erupt.
You **can't/couldn't have** seen John in Australia – he's never been!
I suppose they **might/may/could have** seen a shark. It's possible.

Perfect modals
We use perfect modals (modal + *have* + past participle) to talk hypothetically about the past.
I'm sorry I didn't call; I **should have phoned** you.
I'm so full – I **shouldn't have eaten** so much!
Thanks for your help. It **wouldn't have been** possible without you.
I **would have watched** the film, but I didn't know it was on.
I **could have studied** harder, but I was too lazy.
They **couldn't have arrived** earlier; they got the first train.

Vocabulary

🔊 25 **Places**
beach, coast, desert, forest, hill, jungle, lake, mountain, ocean, river, volcano

🔊 26 **Natural world**
canyon, cave, cliff, coral reef, harbour, riverbank, shore, valley, waterfall
avalanche, drought, earthquake, flash flood, heatwave, landslide, tornado, tsunami, volcanic eruption, wildfire

🔊 27 **Words that are nouns and verbs**
aim, break, challenge, change, decrease (n), decrease (v), demand, film, help, impact (n), impact (v), increase (n), increase (v), name, object (n), object (v), permit (n), permit (v), progress (n), progress (v), rescue, research (n), research (v), surprise, suspect (n), suspect (v)

4 Project

WDYT? (What do you think?) > **What is the best way to enjoy nature?**

TASK: Create a proposal for a place in your country or abroad to be made a Natural Wonder of the World. Film your group presenting your proposal.

Learning outcomes
1 I can make a video proposal to nominate a place to become one of the Natural Wonders of the World.
2 I can use appropriate language from the unit.
3 I can synthesise information.

Graphic organiser → Project planner p119

1 🎥 Watch the video of students presenting their video nomination. Which place did they choose? What country is it in?

STEP 1: THINK ●○○○

2 Read the Model project and match descriptions a–d with paragraphs 1–4.
   a information about what you can do there
   b a short introduction, saying what the video is for
   c a conclusion, summarising what's been said and giving reasons why it's an ideal choice
   d what the place is, where it is, basic facts about it

STEP 2: PLAN ●●○○

3 Think about the video and the Model project. Answer the questions.
   1 What features did the video include to make it attractive?
   2 What else could you add to the video? Where would you add it in the script?

4 Work in pairs. Read the tips in the Super skills box and practise saying the Key phrases with your partner.

CRITICAL THINKING

Synthesising information

Tips

Look at different sources for relevant information.

Make brief notes using keywords so you can compare and contrast the information.

Identify common information and add anything you already know.

Present your arguments in your own words.

Key phrases

We should find at least (four different websites). Let's use (the official website).

We need to find information about (its location and important facts).

What keywords shall we use?

I think for this place, the keywords are …

All the sites (describe how beautiful it is/ explain why it's unique).

How can we say that using our own words?

5 Work in groups of three. Choose a place to nominate and research it. Use the tips and Key phrases in the Super skills box.

STEP 3: CREATE ●●●○

6 Write your proposal. Make sure you use your own words.

7 Prepare a script to present your proposal.

Model project

1 Today we are delighted to present our proposal for a new Natural Wonder of the World. Once you've heard about it, we're sure you'll agree that this unique place deserves to be chosen.

2 You might not have heard of it, but Maligne Lake is in Jasper National Park in Canada. It's a 22-km-long unspoilt lake set in a huge canyon. It is famous for its spectacular views of the Rocky Mountains and its incredible wildlife. Spirit Island, which is in the middle of the lake, is a perfect place to take in the views and thanks to this, it is said to be one of the most-photographed locations in the world. In fact, Apple used a photo of Spirit Island in one of their advertising campaigns, and they couldn't have chosen a more picturesque place!

3 You can explore the lake by boat or get a canoe. If you're feeling even more adventurous, there are hikes all along the shoreline and the surrounding area. There's even the Skyline Trail, which starts at the lake and finishes in the town of Jasper, 44 km away! Of course, there are shorter walks too and you mustn't miss the incredible waterfall which isn't far from the lake. You can see plenty of amazing wildlife, including elk, white-tail deer, grizzly and black bears and moose. Of course, you might prefer to simply relax on the shore and enjoy the views.

4 Maligne Lake is a fantastic example of nature at its best. It has something for everyone: there are different activities to do there, a range of sights to enjoy and the possibility of seeing many different species of animals. For all these reasons, we believe that Maligne Lake is the ideal choice and should be added to the Natural Wonders of the World.

STEP 4: PRESENT

8 Read the *How to …* tips on p119. Then record your proposal.

9 **Peer review** Watch your classmates' videos and answer the questions.
   1 Which place/places did you think was/were the best choices? Why?
   2 What did you like about the proposals? Why?
   3 Which place would you vote for? Why?

4 FINAL REFLECTION

1 The task
Was your proposal organised and attractive?
Did you present your nomination effectively?

2 Super skill
Did you synthesise the information well?

3 Language
Did you use new language from this unit? Give examples.

Beyond the task
Do you think it's important to spend time in nature? How can we protect places so they remain unspoilt?

5 Communicate

WDYT? (What do you think?)

What makes a good communicator?

Vocabulary: reporting verbs; ways of talking; word formation: prefixes

Grammar: reported speech: statements, questions, orders and requests, reporting verbs

Reading: a history essay about ways of sharing news and information

Listening: a podcast about misunderstandings

Speaking: discussing opinions

Writing: a report

Project: a persuasive presentation requesting a travel scholarship

Video skills p61

Real-world speaking p67

Project pp70–71

CAMERA WORLD

camera_world333
Follow

camera_world333 Caption these photos by writing your comments below. We'll publish the most original ones next week. 😊 👍

1,345 likes

Reporting verbs

1 Complete the sentences with the correct form of the reporting verbs in the box.

admit   agree   confirm   deny   insist   refuse

I didn't touch it.
1 She (…) touching it.

It was me. I broke the window.
2 He (…) to breaking the window.

I know it's wet and cold, but we're still going for a walk.
3 They (…) on going for a walk, even though it was raining.

I won't ever help you again.
4 She (…) to help him ever again.

That's decided then. We're going to create a playlist for our coach.
5 They (…) to create a playlist for their coach.

Yes, I'm going to the party.
6 He (…) that he was going to the party.

60

Vocabulary 5

annielouxi 'But the ball was in!' she **complained bitterly**.

pixiejulest 'Where is everyone?' he **cried out in surprise**. Then he saw it was only 6:00 am.

nelltherat 'Shh! You're **whistling out of tune** again!'

bluehatlad He **cheered excitedly** until he realised he was at the wrong concert.

paddy55ok 'Not another pizza party!' she **muttered under her breath**.

lindy321tt 'Shall I tell him he's got his shirt on inside out?' she **whispered softly**.

skater_dani63 'Do something about this rain! It's driving me crazy!' she **shouted at the top of her voice**.

applenancie He was **boasting proudly** about his cooking skills until he dropped everything on the floor.

maxmixtop 'What are you two **quarrelling** so **fiercely** about? Don't tell me you can't agree again?'

lara32cl 'What annoys me about my teammates is that they **gossip continuously**.'

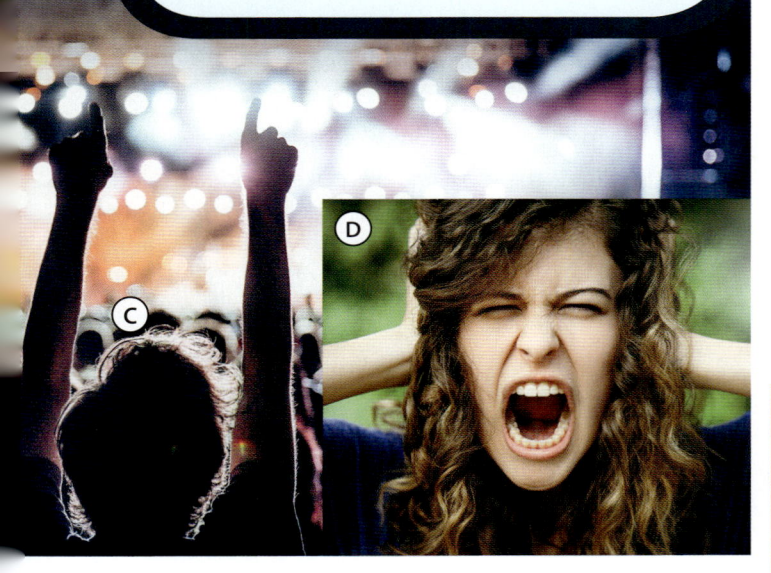

2 🔊 28 Listen to extracts 1–6 and match them with verbs a–f.

a announce *1*
b argue
c claim
d inform
e point out
f report

Ways of talking

3 💬 Work in pairs. Look at the photos. What do you think the people are saying?

4 🎯 Read the captions and check the meaning of the words in bold. Match each photo to one of the comments.

5 Copy and complete the graph with the expressions in bold from exercise 4.

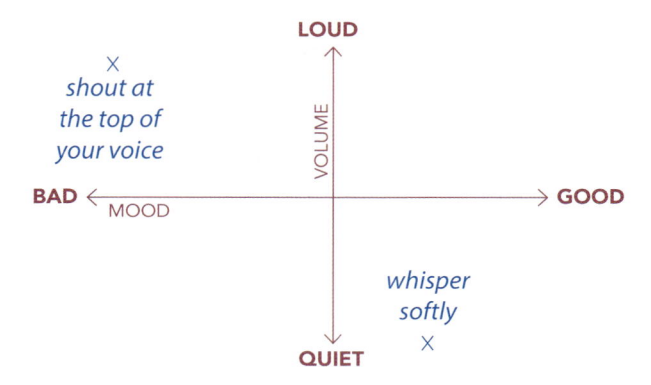

shout at the top of your voice X

LOUD / VOLUME / BAD ← MOOD → GOOD / QUIET

whisper softly X

6 💬 Work in pairs. Ask and answer the questions.

1 When you disagree with something or think something is unfair, do you mutter under your breath or do you complain bitterly?
2 Have you ever boasted proudly about a skill or an achievement? What were you boasting about?
3 Do you know anyone who whistles out of tune? What do you do?
4 When was the last time you shouted at the top of your voice? Why did you shout?
5 Have you ever cheered excitedly? If so, why?
6 Does it bother you if other people whisper softly while you're watching a film? Have you ever told someone to stop whispering?

VIDEO SKILLS

7 🎥 Watch the video. What are the four main topics that the presenter discusses?

8 💬 Work in pairs. Discuss the questions.

1 Who is this video aimed at?
2 Are videos like this more useful than written tips? Why/Why not?

5 Reading and critical thinking

A history essay

1 👥 Work in pairs. How many different ways of sharing news or information can you think of?

Write an article online, send a message …

2 Look at the ways of sharing news in the box. Which ones can you see on p63? Did you think of any of these ways in exercise 1?

> cave painting   chain of signals (smoke, fire or flag)
> human messenger   messenger pigeon
> stone tablet   town crier   whistling

3 Copy and complete the table. What do you think are the advantages and disadvantages of these forms of communication?

	Advantages	Disadvantages
stone tablet		
cave painting	easy to understand	only visitors to the cave can see it
messenger pigeon		
human messenger		
chain of signals		
town crier		
whistling		

4 🔊 29 Read and listen to the essay. Check your ideas in exercise 3. What other advantages and/or disadvantages does the article mention?

5 Read the essay again. What do the numbers refer to?

1 3500 BCE   4 776
2 70   5 5
3 40   6 35,000

6 Complete the sentences in your own words.
1 According to the text, humans are different from other living creatures (…).
2 People think the Kish tablet was the (…).
3 People possibly painted on caves to show (…).
4 The town crier rang a bell and cried 'Oyez' to (…).
5 People on La Gomera whistled to (…).

Subskill: Understanding formal language

We use different words for different types of texts. Some essays and articles use formal words, whereas texts such as chatty blogs or emails to friends use more informal language.

7 **Word work** Look at the formal words in bold in the essay and match them with their less formal equivalent 1–8.
1 short
2 so
3 while
4 but
5 likely to be affected by something
6 seen themselves as different to
7 easy
8 people that live in a place

8 Complete these sentences with one of the formal words in bold in the essay.
1 We needed to send messages over great distances, (…) messenger pigeons were used.
2 English is the most widely spoken language, (…) a great deal more people speak Mandarin Chinese as their native language.
3 Three per cent of the world's (…) speak more than four languages.
4 Americans and the British both speak English. (…), their sign languages are different.

9 👥 Work in pairs. Answer the questions.
1 What are the advantages and disadvantages of using a minority language like Silbo Gomero?
2 Have you/Has anyone you know ever made up a spoken or written language? What did you/they use it for?

CRITICAL THINKING

1 **Understand** Look at the essay again. State your favourite way of sharing news or information in the essay. Explain why.
2 **Analyse** Identify whether this way has been replaced by modern technology. If so, how?
3 **Create** Imagine how this communication method could be developed in the future.

Research

Silbo Gomero is unusual because it uses whistles instead of words. Find out about another unusual language and present your research to the class.

A brief history of SHARING NEWS AND INFORMATION

Humans have always **distinguished** themselves from other living beings through their ability to communicate complicated thoughts and ideas. Nowadays, it is easy to inform the whole world about an event simply by pressing 'send' on our mobile devices, but how did our ancestors spread their news?

Some experts claim that the first form of written communication was the Kish tablet in 3500 BCE, which is a stone carved with symbols. These symbols represented physical objects. However, if we travel back to 35,000 years ago, early humans were painting on cave walls. Many historians have asked themselves why cave people did this and there are several theories: some say these ancestors used paintings to describe hunting expeditions, **whereas** others believe they drew animals to show the difficulties of surviving.

Did you know?
Almost all the residents of La Gomera understand Silbo Gomero and it has been taught as a school subject there since 1999. It's a language and not a secret code (where vowels and consonants are replaced by whistles).

Nevertheless, cave paintings could only communicate a message to someone close by, so it was not useful for broadcasting news further away. In 776 BCE, the Greeks used a messenger pigeon to announce the results of the Olympic Games. About 300 years later, the original marathon runner, Pheidippides, ran about 40 km to Athens to say that they had won a battle at Marathon. Records confirm that they used human messengers in Egypt and China between 200 and 100 BCE. However, living messengers could be slow and **prone to** accidents. Other more immediate responses were needed and as a result, people used signals in chains – smoke, fire or flags. These signals did not always work well, as they depended on humans or weather.

In Medieval England (1066–1485), there was an effective way of making public announcements – a town crier. To gather the crowd, he would ring a bell and shout, 'Oyez, Oyez, Oyez!' which comes from the 13th-century French word 'Oiez!' ('Listen!'). As most town **inhabitants** at that time could not read, the crier would then read out the news, new laws and other announcements.

When Europeans first settled on the Spanish island of La Gomera off the coast of Africa, they discovered that the shepherds there used a whistling language called Silbo Gomero to communicate amongst themselves. In fact, over 70 different groups of people worldwide whistle, from hunters in the Amazon rainforest to Inuit whalers. It requires less effort than shouting or running. It is instant and in open spaces, it can travel up to 5 km.

Thus, when you next click on 'send' to share your news, spare a thought for your ancestors who may not have found this task quite so **straightforward**.

The longer read → Resource centre

5 Grammar

Reported speech: statements

1 Read the example. How do verbs normally change from direct speech to reported speech?

> 'They use paintings to describe the animals that live here', some experts said.
>
> Some experts said that they used paintings to describe the animals that lived there.

2 Copy and complete the table with the tense changes.

Direct speech	Reported speech
present simple	past simple
present continuous	1 (…)
past simple	2 (…)
past continuous	3 (…)
present perfect	4 (…)
past perfect	5 (…)
will	6 (…)
be going to	7 (…)
would	8 (…)
can	9 (…)
must/have to	10 (…)

3 How do words 1–9 change in reported speech?

1. this/these
2. here
3. today
4. yesterday
5. tonight
6. tomorrow
7. next (week/month/year)
8. last (week/month/year)
9. now

4 Complete the second sentence so it means the same as the first.

1. 'We finished our poster last night.'
   They said they had finished their poster the previous night.
2. 'I'm going to arrive late this evening, but I'd like pasta.'
   She said (…) late (…), but that she (…).
3. 'It's raining here now.'
   She said it (…).
4. 'Laura will lend me her bike tomorrow because Leo's mending mine today.'
   He said Laura (…) bike because Leo (…).
5. 'I can help you with the party next Friday.'
   He said he (…) with the party (…).

Reported speech: questions

5 Read the examples and choose the correct option to complete the rules.

> 'Why did people paint on the walls?' you may ask.
> You may ask why people painted on the walls.
> 'Is it easy to learn Silbo Gomero?' she wondered.
> She wondered if/whether it was easy to learn Silbo Gomero.

1. The tenses, pronouns and other words **change/ don't change** in the same way as in reported statements.
2. We **use/don't use** the auxiliary verb *do*.
3. The order of the words **is/isn't** different from direct questions.
4. We use *if/whether* if there **is/isn't** a question word (*What*, *How*, *When*, etc.).
5. We **use/don't use** question marks.

6 Read Freya's questions. What do you think is the matter with Jamie? Rewrite Freya's questions in reported speech.

1. 'What's the matter?' Freya asked Jamie.
   Freya asked Jamie what the matter was.
2. 'When are you playing?' Freya asked him.
3. 'Have you looked in this pile of dirty clothes?' asked Freya.
4. 'Did you also look in the washing machine?' Freya then asked Jamie.
5. 'Was your football shirt there?' asked Freya.

7 Work in pairs. Think of a time when you lost something and asked someone for help. Write a short summary and then compare with your partner.

I lost my … and I asked my best friend if he/she could help me. She/He asked me …

8 Answer the question to solve the Brain teaser.

BRAIN TEASER

Paul was going to the vending machine, so Becca asked him if he could buy her some crisps. When he came back, she asked him how much she owed him. He said that he'd paid €1.10 for the crisps and some chewing gum, but that the crisps had cost €1 more than the gum.

How much did the gum cost?

Vocabulary and Listening 5

Speech bubbles from cartoons:
- What's this?
- It's bean soup.
- I don't care what it's been. I want to know what it is now!
- That's a cute black dog.
- Yes, it's cute. But it's white!

Word formation: prefixes

1 Look at the cartoons. What is the misunderstanding in each one?

2 Match 1–6 with descriptions a–f.
1. An **immature** friend
2. An **irresponsible** family member
3. An **unreliable** interpreter
4. A **dissatisfied** customer
5. A person who tells **inappropriate** jokes
6. An **impolite** person

a often **mistranslates** words.
b **underuses** words like 'please' and 'thank you'.
c might be **disorganised** and **uncooperative** with housework.
d may **overdo** it and upset someone.
e usually feels that the service is **substandard**.
f is generally childish and can be **antisocial**.

> **Word formation: prefixes**
> We use some prefixes to give an opposite or negative meaning, e.g. mature/**im**mature or cooperative/**un**cooperative, or to add an additional meaning, e.g. **mis**translate, **over**do, **under**use, etc.

3 Copy and complete the table with the adjectives in the box to make the opposite or negative meaning. Are there any patterns?

> adequate   appropriate   believable   cooperative
> literate   logical   mature   organised   polite
> regular   reliable   responsible   satisfied   sensitive

dis-	(…)
il-	(…)
im-	(…)
in-	(…)
ir-	(…)
un-	(…)

4 Find the prefixes in the questions. What meaning does each prefix have?
1. Do you replace objects you break even when the owner says it's unnecessary?
2. How often do you prejudge people you don't know? Is this disrespectful?
3. Are you bilingual or even multilingual? If not, would you like to be?
4. Do you tell the cook if the food is undercooked, overcooked, substandard or even inedible?
5. Can you think of some examples of antisocial behaviour?
6. Have you ever read an autobiography? Whose?

5 💬 Work in pairs. Ask and answer the questions in exercise 4.

A podcast

6 🔊 30 Listen to Joe and Bo's podcast about misunderstandings. Which of the situations in exercise 2 do they mention?

7 Answer the questions. Then listen again and check your ideas.
1. What mistake did Bo make when she asked her brother if he could help her?
2. Why did the people laugh after the president told a joke even though they hadn't understood it?
3. Has British singer Adele really got a song about 'chasing penguins'?
4. Why did Shelly and her brother never turn off the radio halfway through a song?
5. Why did Jason ask his mum where all the money was?

▶ **Subskill: Understanding rapid speech**
If speakers are talking rapidly, it may be difficult to catch individual words. Try to understand the overall meaning and then think about what the individual words could be.

8 🔊 31 Listen to extracts from the recording. Complete the sentences with the words you hear.
1. (…), Bo, tell us what happened to you yesterday.
2. Mum and Dad (…) dinner wasn't ready.
3. It was (…) so I apologised.
4. I thought he'd (…) .
5. A president decided (…) audience a joke.
6. If not, how did all those musicians (…) their songs?

Pronunciation: Connected speech: word linking ➔ p117

65

5 Grammar

Reported speech: orders and requests

1 Read the examples and answer the questions.

> 'Please laugh now!' said the interpreter. → The interpreter told everyone to laugh.
>
> 'Can you help me?' I asked my brother. → I asked my brother to help me.
>
> 'Don't worry about it', Dad said. → Dad told me not to worry about it.

1 When do we use *ask* and *tell*?
2 How do we form the negative infinitive?

2 Rewrite the orders and requests in direct or reported speech.

1 'Please don't shout!'
2 She asked me to rewrite the essay because it was illegible.
3 'Would you mind not eating in the car?'
4 My friends often tell me to stop whistling.

Reporting verbs

3 Read examples a–e and match them with verb patterns 1–5.

> a I apologised for not making the dinner.
> b My sister convinced me that Adele was singing about chasing penguins.
> c He'd agreed to help you.
> d He denies agreeing.
> e We invited you to send in funny stories.

1 reporting verb + infinitive
2 reporting verb + object + infinitive
3 reporting verb + verb -ing
4 reporting verb + preposition + verb -ing
5 reporting verb + (object) + *that* + clause

suggest and recommend

He suggested ordering a pizza.
He recommended that we order a pizza.

4 Match the reporting verbs in the box with the correct verb pattern from exercise 3. For some verbs, more than one pattern may be possible.

| admit to   agree   apologise for   ask   convince
| decide   deny   insist on   invite   offer   promise
| refuse   suggest   tell |

5 Complete the second sentence so it means the same as the first. Use the word given in brackets. Do not change the word given.

1 'Would you like to spend the weekend at our farm?'
She invited (…) **(him)** the weekend at their farm.

2 'Why don't you speak more loudly so everyone can hear?' he said.
He suggested (…) **(loudly)** so everyone could hear.

3 'Remember to send a message when you get there!' she said.
She told him (…) **(not)** send a message when he got there.

4 'We'll make the poster. It's our turn', they said.
They (…) **(insisted)** the poster, as it was their turn.

5 'I cried at the end of the film, but don't tell anyone.'
Dad (…) **(admitted)** at the end of the film.

6 Work in pairs. Write three questions beginning 'When did you last … ?' Use verbs in exercise 4. Change pairs. Ask and answer your questions.

> When did you last apologise for being late?

> I apologised for being late for a concert.

7 Find seven more mistakes in the text and correct them.

GRAMMAR ROUND-UP
1 2 3 4 5 **6 7 8**

Advertising as communication

What's the ~~most~~ catchiest advertisement you've ever seen? Did you know that people have promoted their goods for the dawn of time? We know a Roman shopkeeper must has done so, because examples were found in the ruins of Pompeii dating from 79 CE. When TV adverts first appear, they attracted attention by telling us a story. They promised improving our lives. In recent years, adverts had focused on the environment, claiming that their product is greener than the rest. But with the advance of digital technologies, will anyone watching adverts on TV in two years' time? Or will the advertising agencies developed a new approach?

Real-world speaking 5

Discussing opinions

1 🎥 Watch the video. Does Liam need to give Jess good or bad news?

2 Watch again. Complete gaps 1–5 in the dialogue.

3 Watch again. Which Key phrases are not used?

Liam: The venue's just confirmed they're **1** (…) our concert. I have to tell Jess, but I'm not sure how to. She'll be **2** (…) – she was bragging about it yesterday.

Allyson: It's not going to be easy, but you have to tell her.

Liam: I could send her a message. What do you think?

Allyson: I suppose that's the easiest thing to do, but don't you think it's a bit cold? You told me you'd been in the band together for ages.

Liam: I see what you mean, but what if someone else **3** (…) her that it's off before I see her at school tomorrow?

Allyson: You have a point there. Phone her! I'm sure that's the most direct way.

Liam: True, but she always leaves her phone on silent and she said she was **4** (…) to her dance class.

Allyson: Oh. The way I see it, you're going to have to go to the dance studio then. That way you can't **5** (…) her!

Liam: You know, I think you're right.

4 Create your own dialogue. Follow the steps in the Skills boost.

SKILLS BOOST

THINK
Choose a piece of good news to give to someone. Make notes about giving them the news.

PREPARE
Prepare your dialogue. Use the Key phrases for discussing opinions.

PRACTISE
Practise your dialogue.

PERFORM
Act out your dialogue for the class.

5 **Peer review** Listen to your classmates and answer the questions.
1 How did they decide to give the good news?
2 Which Key phrases did they use?

Key phrases

Giving your opinion
I suppose that's …   The way I see it …
I'm sure (that) …

Asking others for their opinion
What do you think?/How do you feel about … ?
What would you say if … ?
But don't you think it's … ?
But what if … ?

Agreeing/Disagreeing
I see what you mean.
You have a point there.
You know, I think you're right.
I suppose so, but …/True, but …/Maybe, but …

🇺🇸💬 US ➡ UK

You have a point there. (US) ➡ You've got a point there. (UK)

Phrasebook ➡ p124   67

5 Writing

RINDALL HIGH SCHOOL WEBSITE

INTRODUCTION
The purpose of this report is to give our opinion on the school website, in particular its organisation, look and content, and also to make suggestions for improvement. In writing this report, I have asked all my classmates in Year 11 for their views.

KEY FINDINGS

Organisation and Look

Eighty per cent agreed that:
- the website was well organised
- the home page looked welcoming
- the website was easy to navigate
- the images made the site look attractive

Nevertheless, around a third commented that the site was slow to load due to the large number of images.

Survey results: 10% / 90%

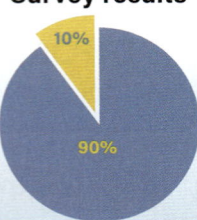

Content

Nine out of ten students surveyed thought that the information for families was well thought-out and included the essentials, for example important dates and information about the staff, school programme and after school clubs.

However, individuals pointed out that they were dissatisfied with the following:
1. there was no mention of events organised by students, for example the charity concert or the photo exhibition
2. the information about other interesting events for students was inadequate
3. some of the information was out of date and needed updating

RECOMMENDATIONS
It was felt by almost everyone that the school should encourage students to create and edit content and design the website. People thought that these fresh ideas might help make the website more appealing. To this end, I would therefore recommend that the school sets up a student club whose principal aim is to develop the website.

A report

1 Read the message on the social media feed. What does the school want students to do? Why?

> **Rindall High School** @RindallHigh
> We'd love more of our students to visit our website so we can hear your opinions about it. Be honest about the organisation and content of the website, and tell us your recommendations for improvements. Together we can make it better for everyone! #BetterTogether

2 Read the report. Copy and complete the table about the website.

	Good points	Bad points
Organisation and look	welcoming home page	
Content		

▶ Subskill: Presenting key findings
Your report should be divided into paragraphs and each one should have a heading. You may use bullet points if you want. Use expressions to describe the website and also to make recommendations.

3 Read the report again and answer the questions.
1. How did the writer choose the heading for each of the paragraphs?
2. What information does the writer include in each paragraph?
3. What techniques does the writer use to present the key findings?

4 Find expressions in the report which we can use to …
1. describe the aim of the report.
2. present key findings.
3. make recommendations.

5 Complete the sentences with expressions from exercise 4. Which section of the report would you find them in?

1 (…) evaluate the school website and offer recommendations for improvement.
2 (…) that the website was user-friendly and attractive.
3 (…) that it was rather disorganised and needs a rethink.
4 (…) that the current website looks unprofessional and needs to be updated.
5 (…) the school employs a professional social media manager to look after the site.

6 Write a report about your own school website or a website you know well. Follow the steps in the Skills boost.

SKILLS BOOST

THINK
Make notes on the organisation, look and content of your own school website or a website you know well and make recommendations. Use the table in exercise 2 to help you. Invent some statistics to back up your ideas.

PREPARE
Organise your notes into paragraphs with a title for each one.

WRITE
Write your report. Use your notes and the useful expressions in exercise 4 to help you.

CHECK
Read your report. Answer the questions.
1 Have you organised your report into logical paragraphs with headings?
2 Have you used the expressions to present the key findings?
3 Have you used some of the vocabulary from this unit?
4 Have you included some examples of reported speech?

7 **Peer review** Exchange your report with another student. Answer the questions.
1 Has the writer organised their report into clear paragraphs with headings?
2 Does the writer present their key findings clearly?
3 Do you agree with their recommendations? Why/Why not?

QUICK REVIEW 5

Grammar

Reported speech: statements
We use reported speech to report something that someone said.
'I **haven't done** my homework'.
She said that she **hadn't done** her homework.
We often change the pronouns, e.g. *you* → *him*, *her* or *they* and time words, e.g. *today* → *that day*
We *say something*, but *tell **someone** something*.

Reported speech: questions
The order of the words in reported questions is different from direct questions.
We don't use auxiliary verbs (*do*, *did*, *have*, etc.).
We use *if/whether* if there isn't a question word.
We don't use question marks.
'Why **was art** important to our ancestors?' you may ask.
You may ask why **art was** important to our ancestors.
'**Is it** a nice language to learn?' she wondered.
She wondered **whether/if it was** a nice language to learn.

Reported speech: orders and requests
We use *ask* to report a request and *tell* to report an order.
We form the negative infinitive with *not to*.
'Can you cook dinner?' I asked my sister. → I **asked** my sister to cook dinner.
'Please smile now!' said the photographer. →
The photographer **told** everyone to smile.

Reporting verbs
Reporting verbs follow different verb patterns.
They'd **agreed to let** you perform.
We **invited you to write** about your best friend.
He **denies taking** your bike.
I **apologised for (not) whistling** loudly in the competition.
My friend **convinced me that** penguins could fly.

Vocabulary

🔊 32 **Reporting verbs**
admit, agree, announce, argue, claim, confirm, deny, inform, insist, point out, refuse, report

🔊 33 **Ways of talking**
boast proudly, cheer excitedly, complain bitterly, cry out in surprise, gossip continuously, mutter under your breath, quarrel fiercely, shout at the top of your voice, whisper softly, whistle out of tune

🔊 34 **Word formation: prefixes**
antisocial, autobiography, bilingual, disorganised, disrespectful, dissatisfied, illiterate, illogical, immature, impolite, inadequate, inappropriate, inedible, insensitive, irregular, irresponsible, mistranslate, multilingual, overcooked, overdo, prejudge, replace, substandard, unbelievable, uncooperative, undercooked, underuse, unnecessary, unreliable

69

5 Project

WDYT? (What do you think?)
What makes a good communicator?

TASK: Give a persuasive presentation on why you should be given a travel scholarship.

Learning outcomes
1 I can create an interesting, well-organised presentation with my classmates.
2 I can use appropriate grammar and vocabulary from the unit in my presentation.
3 I can speak persuasively.

Graphic organiser → Project planner p120

1 Watch a video of students explaining why they should be given a travel scholarship. What reasons do they give?

STEP 1: THINK

2 Work in groups of three. Which of these things do you need to include in your presentation? In what order?
1 your choice of city
2 closing remarks
3 thanks to the judges
4 your personal details
5 reasons you should be chosen for the prize
6 an outline of your presentation

STEP 2: PLAN

3 Work in your groups. Choose the city you'd like to visit and brainstorm reasons why. Make notes about why your group should be chosen.

4 Look at the list in exercise 2 and decide who is going to be responsible for each one.

5 Create the slides and the presentation notes for each slide. Decide who will present each part.

STEP 3: CREATE

6 Work in groups. Read the tips in the Super skills box and practise saying the Key phrases with your group.

COMMUNICATION — SUPER SKILLS

Giving a persuasive presentation

Tips

Speak clearly: don't mutter or whisper, but don't shout either. Don't be afraid to boast!

Try not to read directly from the slides.

Use your body language and gestures to help support your presentation.

Key phrases

We're here today to persuade you that we're the best choice for this scholarship.

After much discussion, we decided …

While other groups may … , we'd like to persuade you that …

There's no doubt that/We'd like to leave you with no doubt that/It can't be denied that/You'd have to agree that …

Over to you, (Scott)/(Scott) will now talk about/It's (Scott's) turn to speak …

7 Read the *How to …* tips on p120 and practise your presentation. Use the tips and Key phrases in the Super skills box.

Model project

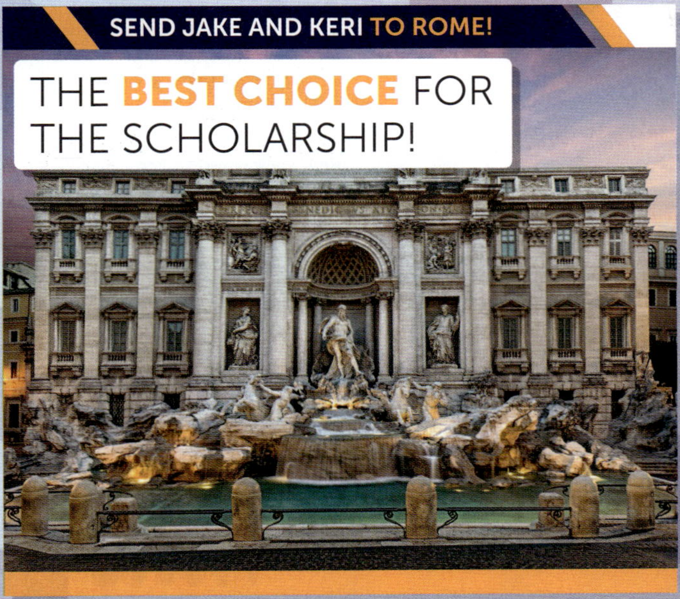

SEND JAKE AND KERI TO ROME!

THE **BEST CHOICE** FOR THE SCHOLARSHIP!

SEND JAKE AND KERI TO ROME!

WHY ROME?
- art students
- see the great museums
- go to classes
- paint historic buildings

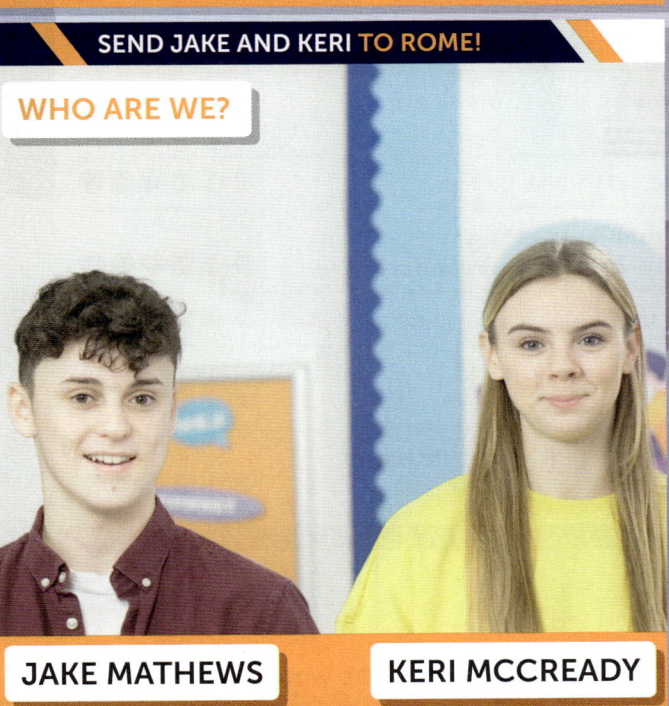

SEND JAKE AND KERI TO ROME!

WHO ARE WE?

JAKE MATHEWS   KERI MCCREADY

SEND JAKE AND KERI TO ROME!

WHY CHOOSE US? WE HOPE TO …
- study art at university
- become better artists
- learn more about art history
- give art classes to everyone when we return
- add to the school blog

STEP 4: PRESENT

8 Present your case to the panel of judges (your classmates) and answer any questions.

9 **Peer review** You are the judges. Listen to the presentations.
   1 Think of one or two questions to ask each group.
   2 Take a class vote. Decide who should win the scholarship and why.

5 FINAL REFLECTION

1 **The task**
   Was your presentation well organised and persuasive?

2 **Super skill**
   Were your group's body language and gestures appropriate?

3 **Language**
   Did you use new language from this unit?

Beyond the task
Think about situations in your daily life at home, with your friends or at school where the wrong body language might lead to a misunderstanding. Share your ideas with the class.

71

6 Challenges

WDYT?
(What do you think?)

What can you do to challenge yourself?

Vocabulary: people; challenges; television

Grammar: conditionals; alternatives to *if*; *I wish* and *If only*; *I wish + would/wouldn't*

Reading: an opinion article about whether we need a rival to be successful

Listening: a radio phone-in programme about TV talent shows

Speaking: checking understanding and clarifying

Writing: an informal article about challenging yourself

Project: a presentation about a TV talent show you have invented

Video skills p73

Real-world speaking p79

Project pp82–83

READY FOR A CHANGE?

You want to **set an objective** or **set goals** … but how likely are you to stick to them? Can you easily **achieve your goals and objectives** or do you **need encouragement**?

1 If I **make a promise**, I always **keep my promise**. I never **break a promise**.   0 1 2 3 4 5

2 I can **overcome a failure** and keep **working on my goals**.   0 1 2 3 4 5

3 When I **make a resolution**, I'm likely to **break my resolution** after a few weeks.   0 1 2 3 4 5

4 I am willing to **take a risk** and try new things.   0 1 2 3 4 5

5 I sometimes **miss opportunities** because I'm scared that if I **take an opportunity**, I'll **be out of my comfort zone**.   0 1 2 3 4 5

6 I **take inspiration** from other people's achievements.   0 1 2 3 4 5

7 My friends help me **deal with setbacks** and **face challenges**.   0 1 2 3 4 5

8 When other people believe I can do things, it **increases my motivation**.   0 1 2 3 4 5

People

1 ♻ Copy and complete the diagram with the words in the box. Can you think of any other words?

| acquaintance   best mate   close friend   colleague   enemy |
| opponent   relative   rival   stranger   teammate |

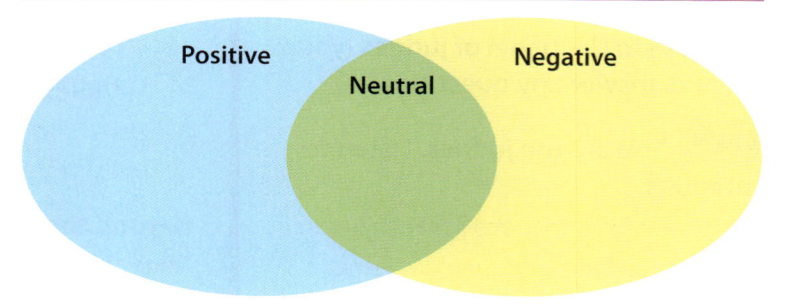

Positive   Neutral   Negative

2 💬 🔊 35 Work in pairs. Listen to the descriptions and match them with people from exercise 1. Then describe the other people to your partner.

Vocabulary 6

3 🗨 **Work in pairs. Ask and answer the questions.**
1 What do you and your best mate like doing?
2 Are you in any teams? If so, do you get on well with your teammates?
3 Did you beat your opponents the last time you played a game or match? What sport/activity was it?

Challenges

4 Look at the photos. What do you think they represent?

5 🎯 Read the quiz and check the meaning of the words in bold. Rate the statements 0–5 (0 = I totally disagree, 5 = I totally agree).

6 Look at the quiz again and find the noun form of the verbs in the box. Which are the same as the verb?

> achieve   challenge   change   encourage   fail
> inspire   motivate   promise   resolve   risk

7 Guess whether your partner agrees (A) or disagrees (D) with the statements.
1 I'm the most out of my comfort zone when I have to speak in class.
2 I never need encouragement to try new things.
3 I need to motivate myself.
4 I'd rather break a resolution than risk failure.
5 If I make a promise to a friend to do something, I'm more likely to keep it than if I promise myself.
6 I enjoy working on my goals and achieving them.

8 🗨 Work in pairs. Ask and answer questions using the ideas in exercise 7. Were your guesses correct?

> When are you out of your comfort zone? Is it when you speak in class?

> No, I'm out of my comfort zone when …

VIDEO SKILLS

9 🎥 Watch the video. Does Ben believe failure is a good or bad thing?

10 🗨 Work in pairs. Discuss the questions.
1 What goal that he has achieved does Ben talk about in this video?
2 Do you think this video is professional or homemade? Why?
3 Videos about 'life lessons' are very popular. Why do you think this is?

6 Reading and critical thinking

An opinion article

1 💬 Work in pairs. What helps people succeed and overcome challenges?

2 Do you think a rival would make you more or less likely to do the things in the box?

> achieve goals   encourage others
> face challenges   increase motivation
> inspire someone   miss opportunities
> overcome failure   set goals/objectives
> take risks   work on goals

3 🔊 36 Read and listen to the article. Do the writers agree or disagree with you?

▶ **Subskill: Finding evidence in the text**

Underline the key words in each sentence, then find and closely read the relevant section in the text. Then:
- look for synonyms, antonyms and paraphrasing
- notice quantifiers (*usually*, *sometimes*, *never* …) and qualifiers (*only*, *totally*, *partly* …) which can change the meaning
- pay attention to negatives, double negatives and negative prefixes
- remember, for a sentence to be true, every part of the sentence must be true

4 Read the Subskill tips. Are sentences 1–6 true or false? Find information in the article to support your answer.
1. Antoni believes having a competitor pushes you to achieve results.
2. People ran more quickly only when they weren't trying to beat an opponent.
3. Certain characteristics of opponents can make us angry because our opponents try to hide them.
4. According to Isabel, one study showed that athletes practised more after they were made to think of a rival.
5. Teamwork usually makes it unlikely that people are not ready to face challenges.
6. Isabel thinks having a rival is unnecessary because we shouldn't compete against others.

5 Which tip(s) helped you answer the questions in exercise 4?

6 Choose the correct answer a–c.
1. Antoni thinks people work harder when …
   a they set tough objectives.
   b their objectives are realistic.
   c their competitors succeed in doing something.
2. Antoni says the positive effects of rivalry …
   a are more noticeable in sports.
   b apply to different situations.
   c have more benefits in the classroom than any other area.
3. Identifying our own negative characteristics …
   a can improve how we feel.
   b doesn't affect our relationships with others.
   c is only possible if they have been hidden before.
4. Research into cooperation has shown that depending on others …
   a increases people's different strengths and talents.
   b boosts our belief in others and our connections with them.
   c means people start to enjoy teamwork more than working individually.

7 **Word work** Match the definitions with the words in bold in the article.
1. believe or recognise that something is good enough
2. trust someone to do something for you
3. achieves, succeeds in doing something
4. didn't consider something
5. a situation in which people or teams compete against each other
6. work with other people to achieve a good result for everyone
7. particular qualities in someone's character

8 💬 Work in pairs. Ask and answer the questions.
1. Whose opinion do you agree with more: Antoni's or Isabel's? Why?
2. Who motivates you to succeed most – other people or yourself? How?

CRITICAL THINKING

1. **Remember** Read the article again. State the main arguments each writer uses.
2. **Evaluate** Think about both arguments and identify your own personal opinion. How does having a rival make you feel? How do you feel about cooperating with others rather than competing with them?
3. **Create** Draw an image, choose a photo or write a paragraph which best shows how you feel about the question (*Do you need a rival to be successful?*). How does your image/paragraph reflect your opinion?

| ABOUT | LATEST POSTS | ARCHIVES | SUBSCRIBE | MORE ▼ |

THE BIG QUESTION: Do you need a rival to be successful?

YES says **Antoni,** because rivals help us achieve our goals.

When you have a rival, it increases your motivation to succeed and can help you achieve far more than you ever imagined. How? Seeing what a rival **accomplishes** makes tough objectives seem more realistic, so you work harder. This effect is well known in sport – if you compete against a rival, you will be more motivated. In fact, one study showed that runners ran a 5 km race 25 seconds faster when competing against a rival. The positive effect of **rivalry** isn't just for sport – it has equal benefits in the classroom and other areas of life. Having a rival can help you to set objectives, keep working on goals and encourage you to dream big. As everyone knows, unless you set objectives, you don't work as hard.

Interestingly, rivals could also help us learn about ourselves. Often, our rivals have **traits** that annoy us and, according to a psychological theory, these might be characteristics of our own personality that we keep hidden. If we identified these traits, it would make us **accept** ourselves more. This can make us happier, more confident and get on better with others.

We need rivals. They bring out the very best in us and inspire us to do better, be better and achieve more than we thought possible. That is success.

💬 5   ♡ 20   ⇄ 9

NO says **Isabel,** because it is better to **cooperate** than compete.

Having a rival can be dangerous – we can become so focused on them that we take unnecessary risks and miss out on opportunities. Recently, researchers found that if athletes were reminded of their rival, they didn't practise as much because they wanted to play straight away to win. They **ignored** the opportunity to get extra experience. They wouldn't have done this if they hadn't been so obsessed with beating their rival. This is just as true in any area of life.

When we cooperate instead of competing, everyone benefits. Everyone has different strengths and talents, and teamwork means individuals can all contribute in different ways. Studies have shown that when people work together, creativity and learning increase. Not only that, but **relying on** others builds trust and improves relationships. People are generally more willing to face challenges and overcome failure when they have the support and encouragement of their teammates. Everyone succeeds and there are no losers.

It is absolutely clear that we do not need a rival to improve. The only person we should compete against is ourselves. Success is doing something better today than you could yesterday.

💬 2   ♡ 12   ⇄ 5

Did you know?
The companies adidas and PUMA were set up by two German brothers, Adi and Rudi Dassler. They built their factories on opposite sides of a town called Herzogenaurach. Luckily, they were both successful!

The longer read → Resource centre

6 Grammar

Conditionals

1 Read the examples and match a–e with rules 1–6. The examples may match more than one rule.

> a I **wouldn't have run** as fast if I **hadn't seen** my rival.
> b If we **identified** these traits, we **would accept** ourselves more.
> c If/When you **have** a rival, it **increases** your motivation to succeed.
> d **Unless** you set objectives, you don't work as hard.
> e If you **compete** against a rival, you **will be** more motivated.

1 Zero conditional sentences talk about facts. We can use *when* instead of *if*.
2 First conditional sentences talk about the **future**, for things that are possible or likely.
3 Second conditional sentences talk about **present** and **future**, for things that are imaginary or unlikely.
4 Third conditional sentences talk about the **past**. We imagine changing the past.
5 *Unless* means *if … not*. It is most often used in first conditional sentences.
6 The *if* clause can come first or second. When it comes first, we separate the two clauses with a comma.

2 Complete the second sentence so it means the same as the first. Use the words in brackets and make any necessary changes.

1 I don't want to go to the cinema if you don't go.
   I won't go to the cinema (…) **(unless)**
2 Drink plenty of water or you will get thirsty.
   You get thirsty (…) **(when)**
3 I think seeing a big spider would make me scream!
   I would scream (…) **(saw)**
4 I'm likely to see Mike later, so maybe I can give him your message.
   I will give Mike your message (…) **(if)**
5 I'm glad I went to the party. I met Sara there.
   I wouldn't have met Sara (…) **(if)**

Alternatives to *if*

> We'll enter the race **providing/provided (that)** we train hard.
> **As/So long as** I work hard, I'll achieve my goals.
> He said he would train me **on the condition that** I practised karate every day.

3 Rewrite the sentences with the words in brackets.

1 My parents may give me permission; if so, I'll apply. **(as long as)**
2 My sister let me borrow her jacket – I had to return it later. **(on the condition that)**
3 We'll go to the mountains if the weather's fine. **(providing that)**
4 You can use my guitar – you must be careful. **(so long as)**
5 I hope I pass my exams, then I'll go to university. **(provided that)**

4 Complete the text with the correct form of the verbs in brackets or one suitable word.

When you **1** (…) **(swim)** in freezing cold water, you **2** (…) **(get)** hypothermia – usually. **3** (…) you get out quite quickly, the water will kill you. However, as **4** (…) as you train correctly, you **5** (…) **(be able to)** swim in very cold water.

Lynne Cox was the first person to swim across the Bering Strait from Alaska in the USA to Russia – an area where the average temperature of the sea was 4°C. If she **6** (…) **(not train)**, she **7** (…) **(not be able)** to do it. If you bought or borrowed her book *Swimming to Antarctica*, you **8** (…) **(learn)** about some of her amazing swimming adventures.

5 Correct the mistakes in the questions.

1 What you do if you had some free time tonight?
2 Where will you go if you will go out at the weekend?
3 If you didn't live in this country, where would you liked to live?
4 If you don't eat any food all day, how you feel?
5 What language would you have studied if you hadn't start learning English?
6 Providing that you had enough money, what do you buy?

6 💬 Work in pairs. Ask and answer the questions in exercise 5.

7 Answer the question to solve the Brain teaser.

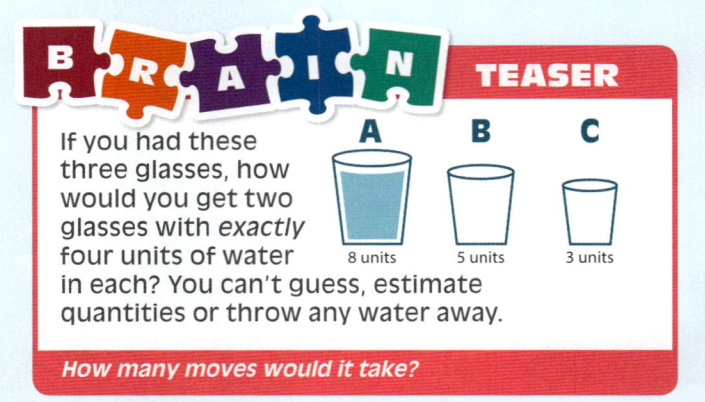

BRAIN TEASER

If you had these three glasses, how would you get two glasses with *exactly* four units of water in each? You can't guess, estimate quantities or throw any water away.

A 8 units B 5 units C 3 units

How many moves would it take?

Pronunciation: Sentence stress in conditionals → p117

Vocabulary and Listening 6

Television

1 Read the text about a TV talent show. Would you like to be in it? Why/Why not?

THE MASKED SINGER

This TV reality singing **competition** has become a huge success. In each series, celebrity **contestants** sing anonymously in elaborate costumes in front of a panel of **judges** and a live audience. Contestants **audition** and **rehearse** in secret. On the show, each contestant **performs** a song and the panel and audience vote on their **performance**. In each episode, there are battles between contestants and the panel tries to guess the **competitors**' identities. Each week, one singer is eliminated and the **presenter** helps them take off their mask! Shows are **broadcast** weekly and it's on catch-up TV. The **producers** are delighted that **viewers** love this TV **entertainment**!

2 Copy and complete the table with the correct form of the words in bold in the text.

Verb	Person	Other nouns
compete	1 *competitor*	2 *competition*
contest	3 (…)	contest
4 (…)	performer	5 (…)
present	6 (…)	presentation
7 (…)	broadcaster	broadcast
entertain	entertainer	8 (…)
judge	9 (…)	judgement
view	10 (…)	viewing
produce	11 (…)	production
12 (…)	–	audition
13 (…)	–	rehearsal

A radio phone-in programme

3 🔊 37 Read the questions. What answers do you think people might give? Then listen. Do the speakers mention any of your ideas?
  1 What singing talent shows do you know of?
  2 What do you think are the good and bad aspects of TV talent shows?
  3 Should there be more music talent shows on TV?

4 Are the sentences true or false? Correct the false sentences.
  1 *The Masked Singer* has been on TV in the UK since 2015.
  2 The contestants know each other's identities, although the judges don't.
  3 One of the presenters really likes the show.
  4 One presenter thinks viewers enjoy guessing the identities most.
  5 Rita Ora wasn't very good at guessing singers' identities.
  6 In Britain, all the contestants were singers in real life.
  7 Kasia got through the audition and went on a show.
  8 In his first audition, Marcos was allowed to choose what to sing.

▶ **Subskill: Inferring meaning**
A speaker's tone and the way they speak often tells you what they really mean. For example, they might hesitate, use flat intonation or emphasise certain words.

5 🔊 38 You will hear phrases 1 and 2 twice. Choose the correct option according to the way the phrase is said in a and then in b. How else could you say the phrases?
  1 'The audition was fun.'
    a I'm sure about this./I'm not certain.
    b I'm sure about this./I'm not certain.
  2 'I learnt a lot from it.'
    a I mean this./I don't really mean this.
    b I mean this./I don't really mean this.

6 🔊 39 Listen to the second part of the programme and answer the questions. How do you know?
  1 Did Kasia and Marcos enjoy their auditions?
  2 Did they learn from their experience?

7 💬 Work in pairs. Ask and answer the questions in exercise 3.

77

6 Grammar

I wish and If only

1 Read the examples and complete the rules.

Present
I wish I was/were good at singing, but I'm not.
Do you wish you could go on the show? You can't.
If only I had a good voice, but sadly I don't.
If only the judges weren't so critical – but they are!
If only they didn't choose such tricky songs. They choose hard ones.

Past
I didn't see the first programme, but I wish I'd seen it.
You went to the audition. Do you wish you hadn't gone?
If only I had been able to choose my own song. I couldn't.
I sang my favourite song. If only I hadn't sung it!

1 We use *wish/if only* + (…) to talk about regrets and things we would like to change about the present.
2 We use *wish/if only* + (…) to talk about past regrets.
3 We use (…) for questions in the present and past.

2 Complete the sentences with the correct form of the verbs in brackets. Which ones are true for you?

1 I can't play any musical instruments. I wish I (…) **(can)** play one!
2 If only I (…) **(not go)** to bed so late yesterday. I wish I (…) **(not be)** so tired now!
3 If only I (…) **(have)** more free time. I haven't got much at all.
4 Our teachers didn't give us any homework last week. I wish they (…) **(give)** us some.
5 My best mate doesn't live near me. If only she (…) **(live)** nearer. I wish I (…) **(not have to)** get a bus to visit her.
6 I forgot to charge my phone last night. I wish it (…) **(work)** now. If only I (…) **(charge)** it.

3 💬 **Work in pairs. Ask and answer questions using the ideas from exercise 2. Ask follow-up questions to find out more information.**

> Do you wish you could play a musical instrument?

> Yes! I wish I could play the guitar. It's been my ambition for ages.

I wish + would/wouldn't

4 Read the examples and complete the rules with *habit*, *object* or *change*.

I wish my friends would stop singing! I can't do my homework.
I wish you wouldn't watch that TV show all the time.

1 We use *wish + would/wouldn't* to talk about something in the present we would like to (…), but can't. This is usually an annoying (…).
2 When we use *wish + would/wouldn't*, the subject and (…) are always different. Usually, the subject is *I*.

5 Rewrite the sentences with *wish* and *would/wouldn't* where necessary.

1 I can't ring my friend because I forgot to bring my mobile.
2 I haven't got much money. I can't go to the cinema tonight.
3 Some people drop litter on the ground – it's so annoying!
4 They forgot to tell me about the party. I didn't know.
5 It makes me angry when my brother uses my computer.

6 Choose the correct option to complete the text.

GRAMMAR ROUND-UP
1 2 3 4 5 6 **7 8**

A TOUGH CHALLENGE

Nepalese climber Nirmal Purja **1 has set/has been setting** a new record for climbing the world's 14 highest mountains – and he's done it in just over half a year, **2 a bit fast/far faster** than anyone else. He **3 used to manage/managed** to complete this tough challenge as part of 'Project Possible'. He climbed Shishapangma, **4 which/where** is over 8,000 m high, an astonishing six months and six days after he **5 was climbing/had climbed** his first mountain, Annapurna in Nepal. He certainly **6 must have/couldn't have** done it any faster! Climbing experts said that fewer than 40 climbers **7 climbed/had climbed** all 14 mountains. What new challenge will Nirmal **8 be doing/have done** at this time next year? Who knows! I can't imagine doing what he did – I don't like heights. I wish I **9 did/had done**. If I had learnt to climb, perhaps I **10 will climb/would have climbed** one of those mountains!

Real-world speaking 6

Checking understanding and clarifying

1 🎥 Watch the video. Which challenge are Simon and Ruth going to do?

2 Watch again. Complete gaps 1–4 in the dialogue.

Owen: Hi! Welcome to Park Challenges.

Ruth: Hi. We'll try the bucket challenge. So, what do we have to do?

Owen: The empty bucket goes down there. And the **1** (…) with the most water in their bucket at the end wins.

Ruth: What? You mean we have to fill that bucket somewhere so we have two full buckets?

Owen: No … What I meant was, you have five minutes to get as much **2** (…) from *this* bucket into *that* one.

Simon: No **3** (…) . We'll just carry it quickly!

Owen: But you can't move either bucket. If you move them, you'll lose. Are you following me?

Ruth: So, you're saying that we have to get water from here to there without moving *either* bucket?

Owen: Yes, that's exactly what I meant.

Ruth: But that's **4** (…) ! If we can't move this bucket, we can't fill that one.

Owen: I wish I could tell you the answer, but I can't. You can complete the challenge any way you want, as long as you don't move the buckets!

3 Watch again. Which Key phrases do you hear?

4 Create your own dialogue. Follow the steps in the Skills boost.

SKILLS BOOST

THINK
Think of a challenge and write notes to explain it.

PREPARE
Prepare your dialogue. Remember to include the Key phrases for checking understanding and clarifying.

PRACTISE
Practise your dialogue.

PERFORM
Act out your dialogue for the class or record it and play it to the class.

5 **Peer review** Listen to your classmates and answer the questions.
1 How well did they do the task?
2 Which Key phrases did they use?

Key phrases

Checking understanding
What do you mean when you say/You mean … ?
If I understand you correctly/So, you're saying that …
You've lost me!/I'm not sure what you mean.
Can you explain again?/Could you go over that again?

Clarifying
What I mean is/What I meant was …
Do you get what I'm saying?/Are you following me?/Do you see what I mean?
Yes, that's exactly what I mean/meant.
No, that's not quite what I meant!

Real-world grammar

If you *move* them, you*'ll lose*.
I wish I *could* tell you the answer.

Phrasebook → p124

79

6 Writing

BRENTON HIGH SCHOOL | Home | About us | Articles | Contact us

Get out of your comfort zone

There's a holiday coming up and you'll be bored … *again!*
What would life be like if you challenged yourself more? Here's your chance to find out – try a challenge! I'd love to hear how you get on.

1 Treat yourself

Get dressed up in your coolest clothes and do something – go to the cinema, go for a smoothie, watch the sunset, do an activity you've always wanted to try … the important thing is to do it by yourself. Making yourself a priority, learning to take care of yourself and finding out what you really love are great ways of developing your independence. Don't miss this opportunity to do something for *you*.

2 Garden or park games

Do you wish you were a bit fitter? A fun way to get some exercise is to invite your friends to some park games. Design competitions and obstacles for teams such as three-legged races, throwing and catching a ball to other teammates using only one hand, or mini bowling … If you do this in the park, make sure you don't disturb other people. Remember to clear up afterwards.

3 Cook a meal

No, I don't mean pizza! The challenge here is to cook a starter, a main course and a dessert using all fresh ingredients. Keep in mind who you are cooking for and cook to impress! Being able to cook at least one incredible meal from scratch is an important life skill.

Take a risk and try one of these challenges – or better still, do all three. If you don't like them, then invent your own. Go for it!

Sam Caton, Year 11

An informal article

1 Look at the article. Who is the writer? Who is the article aimed at?

> **Subskill: Writing for an audience**
>
> When you write an informal article, be clear who the audience is and write appropriately for them. Make the article easy to read and engage the reader. Use semi-formal language and a conversational style.

2 Read the article again. Find examples of features 1–8 for writing an informal article.

1. imperatives to give instructions to the reader
2. humour
3. one or two questions addressed to the reader
4. subheadings and clear paragraphs
5. an ending which links back to the start and/or gives a call to action
6. a title which makes the subject clear
7. something to intrigue the reader and make them keep reading
8. the writer inviting the reader to respond

3 Read the text. How could you make it more appropriate for an informal article? Answer the questions to help you.

TAKE THE OPPORTUNITY TO TOUR A LOCAL FOOTBALL STADIUM

Some people say that touring a football stadium is one of the most interesting things teenagers can do. In my opinion, this is true. On a guided tour, participants learn about the players at the club, the club's history and youth sports programmes. What is more, the shop has a variety of sports clothes. This is a unique opportunity to get an insight into the world of sport.

1. Is the title short and easy to understand?
2. Is the language formal or informal?
3. Does the writer address the reader directly as *you*?
4. Does the writer use a conversational tone and tell the reader what to do?
5. Does the writer use humour?

4 Look at exercise 3 again. Rewrite the text as an informal article. Use the answers to the questions to help you.

5 Write an informal article about three challenges for students at your school. Follow the steps in the Skills boost.

SKILLS BOOST

THINK
A school website or magazine is looking for articles encouraging other students to challenge themselves in fun and inexpensive ways. Think of three challenges and make notes.

PREPARE
Organise your notes into three paragraphs with sub-headings. Think of your title, a short introduction and conclusion. Look at the features of article writing in exercise 2 again and decide where to use at least five of them.

WRITE
Write your article. Use the Model article and your notes to help you.

CHECK
Read your article and answer the questions.
1 Have you tried to make your writing more interesting?
2 Have you used conditional sentences and *I wish/if only*?
3 Have you included appropriate vocabulary from the unit?
4 Have you included at least five of the features from exercise 2?

6 **Peer review** Exchange your article with another student. Answer the questions.
1 Which features from exercise 2 has the writer included?
2 Have they included all the things in the checklist?
3 What do you like about the article? Give reasons for your answer.

QUICK REVIEW 6

Grammar

Conditionals
We use conditionals to talk about situations, real or imaginary, and their consequences.
If/When you **apply** for the show, you **get** an application form.
If you **get** an audition, you'**ll perform** for the judges.
If I **wanted** to improve, I'**d compete** regularly.
If they **hadn't trained** well, they **wouldn't have won**.
Unless you **train** regularly, you **won't win**.

Alternatives to *if*
We can replace *if* with *providing/provided* (*that*), *as long as/so long as* or *on the condition that*. These expressions can go at the beginning of the sentence or in the middle of the sentence.
We will go to the concert **providing/provided (that)** we get tickets.
As long as/So long as I practise every day, I'll be a great guitarist.
She rehearsed the play with me **on the condition that** I helped her make her costume.

I wish and *If only*
We use *I wish* and *If only* to talk about what we would change or what we regret about the present and to express past regrets.
I wish I **didn't have to** get up so early.
I wish I **had gone** to singing lessons before the audition.

I wish + *would/wouldn't*
We use *I wish* + *would/wouldn't* to talk about things we would like to change about the present, but can't. It is often used to talk about annoying habits.
I wish you **wouldn't do** that. It's so annoying!
I wish my friend **would arrive** on time instead of always being late.

Vocabulary

🔊 40 **People**

acquaintance, best mate, close friend, colleague, enemy, opponent, relative, rival, stranger, teammate

🔊 41 **Challenges**

achieve a goal, achieve an objective, be out of your comfort zone, break a promise, break a resolution, deal with setbacks, face challenges, increase your motivation, keep a promise, make a promise, make a resolution, miss an opportunity, need encouragement, overcome a failure, set an objective, set goals, take a risk, take an opportunity, take inspiration, work on a goal

🔊 42 **Television**

audition, broadcast, broadcaster, compete, competition, competitor, contest (n), contest (v), contestant, entertain, entertainer, entertainment, judge, judgement, perform, performance, performer, present, presentation, presenter, produce, producer, production, rehearsal, rehearse, view, viewer, viewing

81

6 Project

WDYT? (What do you think?)

What can you do to challenge yourself?

TASK: Give a presentation about a TV talent show that you have invented.

Learning outcomes
1 I can give an engaging presentation.
2 I can use appropriate grammar and vocabulary from the unit in my presentation.
3 I can use my creativity skills to develop and implement new ideas.

Graphic organiser → Project planner p120

1 🎥 Watch a video of students giving a presentation. What kind of TV talent show are they talking about?

STEP 1: THINK ◼◻◻◻

2 Look at the Model project and answer the questions.
1 Who are the contestants?
2 Who will the audience be?
3 What is the aim of the show for contestants?
4 What do the contestants have to do?
5 What are the show's key selling points (KSPs)?
6 What will the format of the show be?

3 Look at the different types of TV shows in the box and answer the questions.

> business/entrepreneurship   cookery/baking
> dance   design   fashion   learning   make-up
> music/singing   other talents   quizzes
> sport/fitness   survival   travel

1 Are there any others you would include?
2 Which are the most/least interesting? Why?
3 What talent shows do you know of for each type? What do you like/dislike about them?
4 What do you think is the best talent show on at the moment? What is the show's format?
5 Which shows, if any, are aimed at teenagers and/or have teenage contestants?

STEP 2: PLAN ◼◼◻◻

4 Work in pairs. Read the tips in the Super skills box and practise saying the Key phrases with a partner.

CREATIVITY — SUPER SKILLS

Developing and implementing new ideas

Tips
Think of as many ideas as possible and choose the best idea.
Research the show's format.
Test the idea. Do people react positively to it?

Key phrases
How exactly will the show work? What makes it original?
Who will the audience be?
What will contestants have to do/win?
We should ask (six) people what they think of the show format.
How can we improve our show?

5 In your groups, choose a type of show and make notes on your idea. Use the tips and Key phrases in the Super skills box.

Grammar and Vocabulary → Quick review p81

Model project

A INTRODUCTION

We're Billie, Scott and Ash.
Presentation:
- description of the show
- who the show's for and target audience
- the KSPs
- question time

C KSPs

- different type of music reality show
- talented teens write hit songs
- big name rappers, writers and producers give one-off master classes
- cameras show the creative process

B TITLE

RAP STARS

WHO?
- **Contestants:** all 14–18-year-olds
- **Audience:** everyone who loves rap, especially teenagers

WHAT?
- write an original rap
- perform song in front of panel of celebrity judges from the industry
- audience and judges vote on best song
- one contestant eliminated weekly over six weeks

D PRIZE

- the song writer meets the producer and helps produce the song
- the winning song is recorded by a famous rap artist

STEP 3: CREATE

6 Read the *How to …* tips on p120 and choose at least five.

7 Create your presentation using the tips and decide who is presenting each part.

STEP 4: PRESENT

8 Practise your presentation in your groups. Then present your show to the class.

9 **Peer review** Listen to the other presentations and answer the questions.
  1. Which show/s would you want to watch? Why?
  2. Which presentation makes you want to take part as a contestant or judge? Why?

6 FINAL REFLECTION

1 The task
Was your presentation well organised?
Was it engaging?

2 Super skill
Did you develop and implement new ideas?

3 Language
Did you use any new language from this unit? Give examples.

Beyond the task
Why do you think it's important to continually challenge ourselves?

7 Going unplugged

WDYT? (What do you think?)

Could you unplug for a day, a week, a month or even longer?

Vocabulary: lifestyle; chilling out, getting active; expressions with *make* and *do*

Grammar: the passive; the passive: modal verbs; *have/get something done*

Reading: an article about being off the grid

Listening: an informal conversation while trying to get to a place

Speaking: giving directions

Writing: a for-and-against essay

Project: a proposal for an Unplugging Day

Video skills p85

Real-world speaking p91

Project pp94–95

CHILL OUT!

Are you always on the go? Do you need to **take some time out** to relax? Have you considered **putting your feet up** to **recharge your batteries**? Go on, **take a breather** – you deserve it!

Lifestyle

1 Look at the adjectives in the box. Which ones could you use to describe the photos?

> conventional   dull   exhausting   harmful   hectic   inspiring   physically active   satisfying   stressful   thrilling

2 Work in pairs. Which of the adjectives in exercise 1 would you use to describe your lifestyle? Can you think of any more to describe it?

> I think I lead a fairly conventional lifestyle because …
>
> I wish I were more physically active, but …

84

GET ACTIVE!

Fancy **getting involved in** something new? **Take** more of **an interest in** your physical condition by **signing up for** a fitness course. **Keep in shape** and **strengthen your muscles and bones** at the same time!

Chilling out, getting active

3 Check the meaning of the words in bold in the texts. Copy and complete the diagram with the words in the texts and the box.

> be energetic and lively   calm down
> disconnect   drop out (of)
> get into (a new activity)   sit back and relax
> take it easy   take your mind off (something)

Chilling out
take time out

Both
take an interest (in)

Getting active

Vocabulary 7

4 Match definitions 1–6 with expressions from exercise 3.
1 start enjoying a new activity
2 stop thinking about something unpleasant
3 have a lot of energy and be active
4 take a short rest, normally after exercise
5 to make parts of your body more powerful
6 rest after being busy so that you're ready to start again

5 🔊 43 Listen to five different people speaking. What new activity has each one taken up? Why?

6 Complete the questions with the expressions in the box.

> calm down   drop out of   keep in shape
> put your feet up   sign up for

1 When did you last (…) a new activity? What was it?
2 Have you ever had to (…) an activity because you didn't have time to do it?
3 When you're feeling nervous, what kinds of things do you do to (…)?
4 At the end of a school day, do you usually (…) before doing your homework?
5 What physical activity do you do to (…)?

7 💬 Work in pairs. Ask and answer the questions in exercise 6.

VIDEO SKILLS

8 🎥 Watch the video. What does Mon miss most about social media?

9 💬 Work in pairs. Discuss the questions.
1 In the end, does Mon think social media has a positive or negative impact?
2 Do you think you could do something similar to Mon's challenge? What would you find difficult?

85

7 Reading and critical thinking

An article

1 💬 Work in pairs. Look at the photos and the title of the article. What do you think the words in the box might mean?

> full-blown adventure   microadventure
> microbreak   unplugging

2 🔊 44 Read and listen to the article. Check your answers to exercise 1.

3 Answer the questions in your own words. Then read the article again and check your answers. Find evidence to support them.
1 Why do people participate in the National Day of Unplugging?
2 How do we know that unplugging helped some people do more in a day?
3 Why does the article suggest you put your phone in a 'sleeping bag'?
4 What kind of adventure does the article suggest for people who can get away for a while?
5 According to the article, how can you go on an adventure near where you live?
6 According to the article, why should you stop to have a drink while you're studying?

4 **Word work** Match the definitions with the words in bold in the text.
1 live without electricity
2 a telephone that isn't a mobile phone
3 a method for doing something
4 not doing something as big
5 an area of land where people do not usually live
6 when something removes your attention from what you are doing

5 Complete the sentences with one of the words in exercise 4 in the correct form.
1 My mobile's out of battery, so ring me on the (…).
2 I often leave my phone face down so I don't get (…) by the messages.
3 We try to go everywhere by bike – that's our favourite (…) of transport.
4 Organising a week of events is too much; try doing something (…).
5 We're going to (…) when we go camping – no phones, no electricity, no nothing!
6 We spent last summer touring the (…) in Iceland. We didn't see anyone for kilometres.

▶ **Subskill: Referencing**
We use words like *so*, *it* or *there* to refer **back** or refer **forward** to people, things, ideas, etc. This avoids repetition of the same words, sentences or even paragraphs. It's important to understand what these words are referring to so that you can fully understand the text.

6 What do the following words refer to? Choose the correct answer a–c.
1 'doing so' in line 3
   a disconnecting   b having a celebration
   c taking the selfie
2 'this' in line 11
   a getting outdoors   b using the house phone
   c the National Day of Unplugging
3 'there' in line 16
   a being solo   b in the cabin
   c being off the grid
4 'that' in line 19
   a a microadventure   b being close to home
   c a big adventure
5 'latter' in line 25
   a conventional breaks   b microadventures
   c microbreaks
6 'former' in line 26
   a conventional breaks   b microadventures
   c microbreaks

7 💬 Work in pairs. Answer the questions.
1 Had you heard of the National Day of Unplugging before you read this article?
2 Would you like to go on a microadventure? What would you do?

CRITICAL THINKING

1 **Understand** List the advantages and disadvantages of unplugging for a day.
2 **Apply** Examine whether you and the people you know would benefit from unplugging. How could you persuade others to do this?
3 **Create** Complete the phrase 'I unplug to …' in no more than five words to express your reasons to the class. Then create a poster.

ARE YOU READY TO UNPLUG?

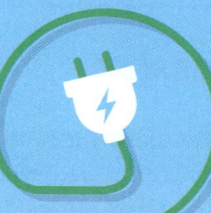

The National Day of Unplugging is celebrated annually in many countries worldwide. People disconnect from technology and send in their selfies explaining their reasons for doing so. These range from the concrete ('to read the newspaper' or 'to get involved in charity work') to the more abstract ('to take a breather' or 'to focus on the things that matter most'). Research seems to support these reasons. One study concluded that after taking time out from technology, participants reported that their days had been more productive: they had revised for exams, spoken to their friends more and even finished a novel. Some said they felt like they were on holiday!

There's no need to wait until this day comes around again to switch off. Some young people choose not to own a mobile phone at all. They use the **landline** to contact friends and instead of looking at social media, they get active outdoors. Do you want to give this a go **on a smaller scale**? Store your phone in a 'mobile phone sleeping bag' so that you won't be **distracted** when it lights up. If you're being disturbed by your larger devices, lock them in a box with a lid.

Now that's done, you'll have time for an adventure! If you can afford to **go off the grid** for longer than a day, consider spending time with your family in a remote cabin. Your adventure doesn't have to stop there; this stay could be preparation for a long-distance hike, such as the Camino de Santiago in northwest Spain. But if you're up for a complete change of lifestyle, you could find your inspiration in 17-year-old Maddie Roark, who grew up in the **wilderness**.

However, if that isn't your thing or you simply don't have the time, why not try a microadventure? What distinguishes this from a full-blown adventure is that they're enjoyed close to home. Try a new **means** of transport. Get yourself a bike, monocycle or scooter and explore your town from a new perspective. If you live near water, paddle boarding and kayaking are great ways to discover the shoreline.

For those of you not ready to commit to a full day, try microbreaks. These should be short and regular, but they shouldn't be confused with conventional breaks. While the latter have often been built into our timetables, we often ignore the former. These unscheduled opportunities allow our bodies to recover. Turning your head away from your screen and taking your fingers off the keyboard to fetch some water give your eyes and wrists a rest.

Whether it's done once a year or on a regular basis, we're sure you'll find your time unplugged satisfying. What's more, both your mind and body will thank you!

Did you know?
Earth Hour is celebrated on the last Saturday of March every year. First organised in Sydney in 2007, the lights are now switched off in more than 180 countries all over the world to show support for the planet.

7 Grammar

The passive

1 Read the examples and complete the rules.

> The National Day of Unplugging **is celebrated** annually in many countries worldwide.
> You **won't be distracted** when it lights up.
> You**'re being disturbed by** larger devices.

1. We form the passive with the correct tense of the verb (…) + (…) participle.
2. We often use the passive to focus on the person or thing affected by the action and not the person or thing that does it.
3. If we want to say who or what does the action, we use the preposition (…) .

2 Read the sentences. Identify the tense of the verb in bold and then rewrite the sentences in the passive.

1. Someone always **interrupts** me when I am reading.
2. They**'re opening** more and more phone shops in my town.
3. Somebody **has scratched** my new bike.
4. Somebody **took** my phone charger by mistake.
5. Our teacher **was recording** our presentations yesterday.
6. Dinner wasn't great last night. Someone **hadn't cooked** the chicken properly.
7. They**'ll hold** an Unplugging Day in my school next month.
8. They**'re going to build** a new shopping centre near my school.

3 Read the information. Write three questions with *get* for your partner. Use the words in the box or your own ideas.

> **get**
> We can use *get* instead of *be* in the passive with active verbs, especially in expressions such as *get distracted*, *get invited* or *get hurt*. We can't use *get* with state verbs:
> *He gets/is invited to parties because he's liked by everyone.* (not ~~he gets liked~~)

| broken | distracted | hurt | invited | offered | paid |

4 💬 Work in pairs. Ask and answer your questions.

5 Complete the text with the correct passive or active form of the verbs in brackets.

Most people **1** *are connected* **(connect)** 24/7. I mean, from the moment we **2** (…) **(wake up)**, we **3** (…) **(check)** social media to see if a new message **4** (…) **(post)**, tickets for our favourite band **5** (…) **(put on)** sale or if someone **6** (…) **(ask)** us something. The truth is, a lot of us **7** (…) **(spend)** more time on screens than we do asleep! That's why some people **8** (…) **(choose)** to disconnect completely for one day a week and to be online 24/6 instead.

6 Complete the questions in the quiz with the correct active or passive form. Then answer the questions.

AllTriviaQuestions

SPORT | HISTORY | SCIENCE | MUSIC
LITERATURE | FOOD AND DRINK

Get Active Trivia

1. When (male cheerleaders / first / introduce) at a Super Bowl?
   1958   1997   2019   never
2. Which (country's team / play) in every World Cup tournament?
   Germany   England   Brazil   Italy
3. Where (the 2028 Olympics / hold)?
   Madrid   Los Angeles   Beijing   Buenos Aires

> **Research**
> Choose a category and research some information. Write five trivia questions for your classmates.

7 Answer the question to solve the Brain teaser.

BRAIN TEASER

Before Jupiter was discovered, what was the largest planet in our solar system?

88

Vocabulary and Listening 7

The Rocks Market, Sydney

Expressions with *make* and *do*

1 Work in pairs. Check the meaning of the words in bold in the quiz. Choose the correct option (A or B). Do you agree with the answer?

Could you **do without** your phone?

You're lost in the middle of the woods. Your phone has run out of battery, you've eaten all your food and your friend has **made off with** the map. What do you do next?

A Sit back and relax, **do up** your jacket to stay warm and **make up** some songs to pass the time. The rescue team will find you eventually.

B Try to **make out** the nearest village. People generally live in valleys or near a water supply, so **make for** a river or stream and follow that downhill.

If your answer is …
A: You're a careful person who prefers to play it safe. You trust that others will find you.
B: You are a more restless person who prefers to take risks and sort out your problems for yourself.

Expressions with *make* or *do*

There are many phrasal verbs and common expressions with *make* and *do*. Most expressions which talk about activities, work or obligations usually take *do*, e.g. *do sport/homework/an exam*, whereas those which relate to creating or producing something often take *make*, e.g. *make a cake/a noise/an excuse*.

2 Copy and complete the table with the words in the box.

a mistake   a point   a school subject/degree
an effort   fun of   harm/damage (to)   nothing
sure   the most (of)   up your mind (to do)
you good   your best

Make	Do
an effort	your best

An informal conversation

3 🔊 45 Listen to the recording. What can you see and do in the places in the box?

Sydney Opera House   Hyde Park   The Rocks Market

4 Correct the information in the sentences. Then listen again and check your answers.

1 Anna turned off her phone and couldn't turn it on again.
  Anna's phone turned itself off and it couldn't be turned on again.
2 Eating and drinking is banned in Hyde Park because visitors are inconsiderate with their rubbish.
3 Flying foxes help spread plant seeds and pollen, but they can't fly very far.
4 The First Nations dance competition is for dancers from all over the world.
5 Handmade jewellery, clothes and crafts are sold at The Rocks Market, but Andy doesn't think much of the street food.
6 Anna and Marcus will have to take a taxi from The Rocks Market to the Opera House.

▶ **Subskill: Understanding words from context**

If you hear a word you don't recognise, try to understand the meaning from context. Then listen to that part again, write down the word(s) you didn't understand and check the meaning.

5 🔊 46 Listen to extracts from the recording. Match words 1–5 with meanings a–g. There are two meanings you do not need.

1 landmark   *c*
2 bound to be
3 harbour
4 stunning
5 creepy

a extremely beautiful
b a place which is safe for boats to stay
c a recognisable building or place
d will almost certainly happen
e the sea
f scary
g unattractive

6 Work in pairs. Discuss the questions.

1 Would you like to spend a week in Sydney? Why/Why not?
2 Do you prefer to be energetic and lively on holiday or take it easy?

Pronunciation: Word stress: expressions with *make* and *do* → p117

7 Grammar

The passive: modal verbs

1 Look at the examples, then complete the rule.

> Active: They **should ban** plastic bottles.
> Passive: **Plastic bottles should be banned**.
> Active: You **can't miss** the street food.
> Passive: **The street food can't be missed**.
> Active: Anna **couldn't turn** on **her phone** again.
> Passive: **Anna's phone couldn't be turned** on again.

To form the passive form of a modal verb, we use the modal verb + (*not*) + (…) + past participle.

2 Rewrite the sentences in the passive.
1. Someone should ban loud music on beaches.
   Loud music on beaches (…) .
2. You can't scratch diamonds.
   Diamonds (…) .
3. You mustn't open these presents before your birthday.
   These presents (…) before your birthday.
4. People must close this gate at all times.
   (…) at all times.
5. The bike shop couldn't repair your bike.
   (…) .

3 Write complete sentences in the passive.
1. High school students (**should allow to start**) school after 10:00 am.
2. Primary school students (**should not give**) any homework.
3. All types of exams (**must ban**) immediately.
4. Promises (**mustn't ever break**).
5. Most online information (**can trust**).

have/get something done

4 Read the examples and choose the correct option to complete the rule.

> Anna only **had** her phone **repaired** last week.
> Marcus **will need to get** the battery **replaced**.

1. Anna **repaired/didn't repair** her own phone. She **went/didn't go** to a repair shop.
2. Marcus **will replace/won't replace** the battery himself. He **will ask/won't ask** someone to do it for him.
3. We can use *have* or *get* + object + past participle to say someone does something for us. '*Get*' is **more/less** formal than '*have*'.

5 Write complete sentences with the correct form of *have* or *get something done*.
1. I (**cut my hair**) last week.
2. I (**check my teeth**) every six months.
3. We (**not redecorate our house**) next week.
4. Sam (**deliver food shopping**) every week.
5. My parents (**just repair their car**).
6. Our class (**take our photo**) last week for the school website.

6 Rewrite the sentences in exercise 5 so they are true for you.

7 💬 Work in pairs. Write questions for the sentences in exercise 5. Then ask and answer.

> When did you last have your hair cut?

> I had it cut two months ago. What about you?

8 Choose the correct option.

GRAMMAR ROUND-UP
1 2 3 4 5 6 7 **8**

A HOLIDAY OFF THE GRID

If only our lives **1 are/were** less stressful and we **2 have/had** more time to take it easy. We suggest **3 that you choose/you to choose** one of our unique destinations to help you recharge your batteries.

THE CANADIAN ROCKIES
Escape into the wilderness to a place which is not as far away **4 as/than** you might imagine. In just over three hours from the airport, you **5 're sitting/'ll be sitting** outside your cabin in the middle of stunning scenery. The mobile phone reception is poor, so you'll **6 force/be forced** to spend time with your companions.

YURTS IN CORNWALL, UK
You **7 mustn't/don't have to** travel halfway across the world to take time out. Cable TV and electricity **8 haven't/hadn't** been installed here, but the wood-burners in these yurts will keep you warm at night. For those **9 which/who** are into wildlife, you'll find many birds by the river. The best surfing beaches are less than 10 km away and in case you're thinking 'I **10 should have brought/should had brought** my beach things', there is a town for shopping about 24 km away.

Real-world speaking 7

Giving directions

1 🎥 Watch the video. Where does Allyson want to go?

2 Watch again. Complete gaps 1–4 in the dialogue.

3 Watch again. Which Key phrases do you hear?

Allyson
Sorry to bother you, but I'm looking for a baseball field.

Customer
I'm afraid I can't help you. I'm not from around here.

Allyson
Excuse me! Do you know this area?

Server
Yeah! I grew up just around the corner.

Allyson
Awesome! I was told there's a baseball field near here.

Server
Yeah, that's right. Head over that way to the **1** (…) . Turn left and then keep walking until you see **2** (…) on your right.

Allyson
I think I saw that on my way down here.

Server
Yeah! If you cut through it, you'll come out next to **3** (…) . Walk around it and you'll end up by **4** (…) . The field is on your left.

Allyson
Cut through the market, walk around the park and the field is on the left.

Server
That's right! You can't miss it!

Allyson
Thanks so much for your help!

Server
You're welcome! Have a great day!

4 Create your own dialogue. Follow the steps in the Skills boost.

SKILLS BOOST

THINK
Decide on a final destination. Make notes on how to get to this place from your school.

PREPARE
Prepare your dialogue. Don't forget to use some of the Key phrases.

PRACTISE
Practise your dialogue. Remember to use hand gestures to make your directions clearer.

PERFORM
Act out your dialogue for the class.

5 **Peer review** Listen to your classmates and answer the questions.
1. How clear were the directions?
2. How many Key phrases did your classmates use?

Key phrases

Asking for directions
Sorry to bother you, but I'm looking for …
Excuse me! Do you know this area?
Can you tell me/Do you know the way to … ?

Being unable to help
I'm afraid I can't help you. I'm not from around here.

Giving directions
Go back the way you came to the …
Turn left/right and keep walking until …
… is on your left/right.
Cut through … / Walk around the … /
Go across the … / You'll end up/come out by …
You can't miss it!

🇺🇸 **US** → **UK** 🇬🇧

field (US) → pitch (UK)

Phrasebook → p125

7 Writing

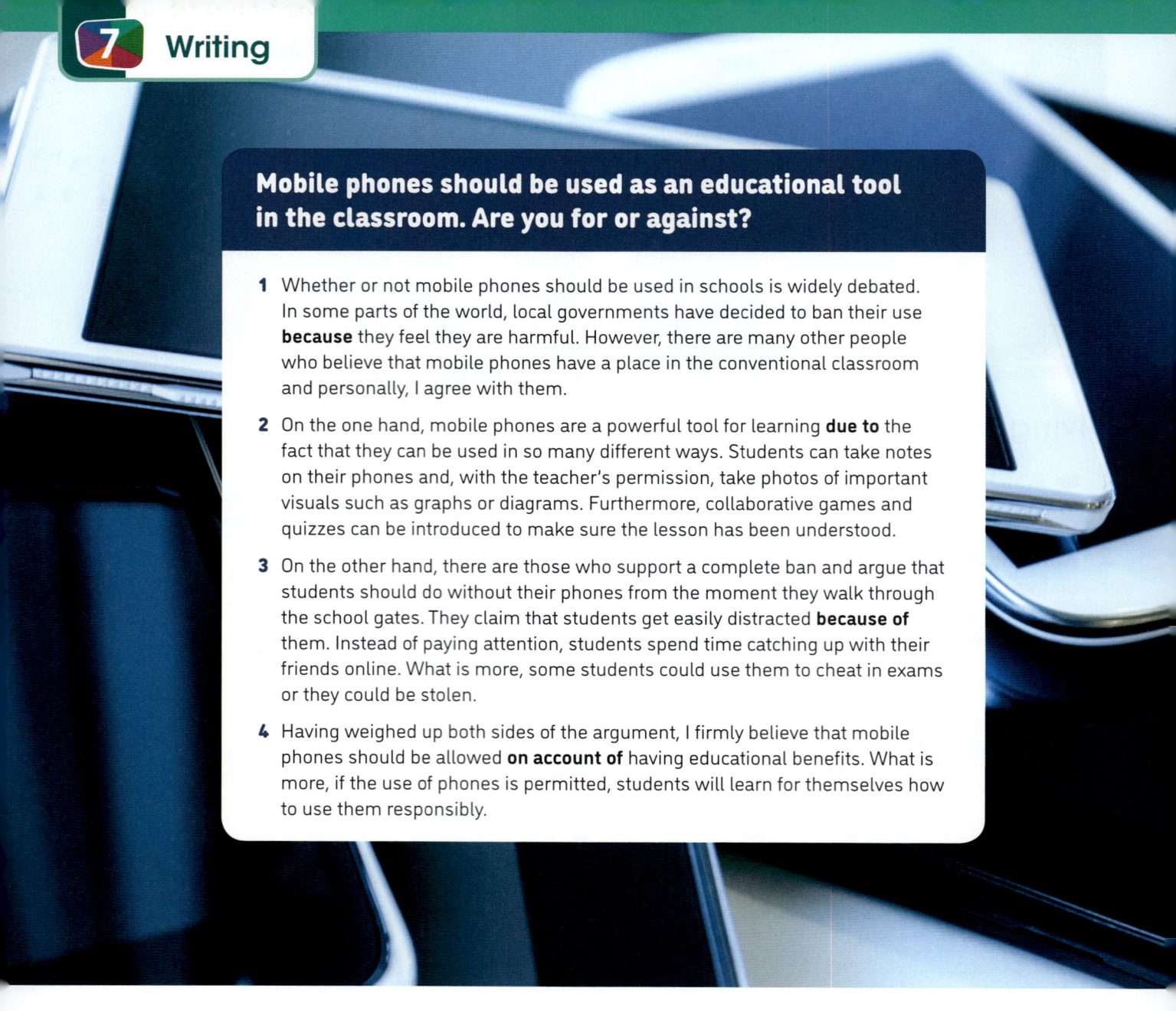

Mobile phones should be used as an educational tool in the classroom. Are you for or against?

1 Whether or not mobile phones should be used in schools is widely debated. In some parts of the world, local governments have decided to ban their use **because** they feel they are harmful. However, there are many other people who believe that mobile phones have a place in the conventional classroom and personally, I agree with them.

2 On the one hand, mobile phones are a powerful tool for learning **due to** the fact that they can be used in so many different ways. Students can take notes on their phones and, with the teacher's permission, take photos of important visuals such as graphs or diagrams. Furthermore, collaborative games and quizzes can be introduced to make sure the lesson has been understood.

3 On the other hand, there are those who support a complete ban and argue that students should do without their phones from the moment they walk through the school gates. They claim that students get easily distracted **because of** them. Instead of paying attention, students spend time catching up with their friends online. What is more, some students could use them to cheat in exams or they could be stolen.

4 Having weighed up both sides of the argument, I firmly believe that mobile phones should be allowed **on account of** having educational benefits. What is more, if the use of phones is permitted, students will learn for themselves how to use them responsibly.

A for-and-against essay

1 Read the title of the essay and then copy and complete the table with your own ideas.

Reasons for	Reasons against
check facts online	get distracted easily

2 Read the essay and answer the questions.
1 Is the writer for or against using phones as an educational tool?
2 What is the main difference between a for-and-against essay and an opinion essay?

3 Match descriptions a–d with paragraphs 1–4.
a arguments for
b arguments against
c conclusion which restates your opinion
d introduction which states your opinion

▶ **Subskill: Using connectors of reason**

We can use words like *because*, *because of*, *due to* and *on account of* to introduce reasons to support our arguments. *Due to* and *on account of* are more formal.

4 Look at the connectors of reason in bold in the essay. Copy and complete the table. What follows each one: a clause, a noun or something else?

Mobiles should be allowed in the classroom …

1 (…)	they have numerous educational benefits
2 *due to*	the fact (that) they have numerous educational benefits
(…)	their numerous educational benefits
(…)	having educational benefits

5 Match 1–4 with a–d to make sentences. Then complete the sentences using the connectors *because, because of, due to* or *on account of*.

1 Some people are unable to fall asleep …
2 Notifications should be switched off …
3 We should avoid screens an hour before bed …
4 Family relationships are neglected …

a the fact that they are distracting.
b the amount of time we spend online.
c looking at too much information online.
d they do damage to our sleep patterns.

6 Write a for-and-against essay to answer the question: *Should technology be removed from our bedrooms?* Follow the steps in the Skills boost.

SKILLS BOOST

THINK
Read the question carefully and decide if you agree or disagree. Copy the table in exercise 1 and complete it for this question. Think about a final argument for your conclusion.

PREPARE
Organise your essay into four paragraphs.

WRITE
Write your for-and-against essay. Use the Model essay and your notes to help you.

CHECK
Read your essay and answer the questions.
1 Have you organised your essay into logical paragraphs?
2 Have you used connectors of reason correctly?
3 Have you used some of the vocabulary from this unit?
4 Have you included some examples of passives?

7 **Peer review** Exchange your essay with another student. Answer the questions.
1 Has the writer organised their essay into clear paragraphs?
2 Does the writer state both sides of the argument?
3 Do they clearly state their own opinion? Do you agree with it?

QUICK REVIEW 7

Grammar

The passive
We use the passive to focus on the object or the person who is affected by the action, and not the person or thing that does it.
Mobile phones **aren't used** on the National Day of Unplugging.
My phone **will be switched** off at 10:00 pm tonight.
My laptop **isn't being repaired** at the moment.
The class **has been cancelled** this week.

The passive: modal verbs
Mobile phones **should be banned** in class.
The market **can't be missed**.
The flying foxes **couldn't be seen** last night.

have/get something done
We can use *have* or *get* + object + past participle to say that someone does something for us.
Elena **had** the screen of her mobile phone **replaced** last week.
Liam will need to **get** his car **repaired**.

Vocabulary

🔊 47 **Lifestyle**
conventional, dull, exhausting, harmful, hectic, inspiring, physically active, satisfying, stressful, thrilling

🔊 48 **Chilling out, getting active**
be energetic and lively, calm down, disconnect, drop out, get into (a new activity), get involved, keep in shape, put your feet up, recharge your batteries, sign up for a course, sit back and relax, strengthen muscles and bones, take a breather, take an interest (in), take it easy, take time out, take your mind off (something)

🔊 49 **Expressions with *make* and *do***
do a degree, do a school subject, do damage, do harm, do nothing, do up, do without, do you good, do your best, make a mistake, make a point, make an effort, make for, make fun of, make off with, make out, make sure, make the most of, make up, make up your mind

7 Project

WDYT? (What do you think?)

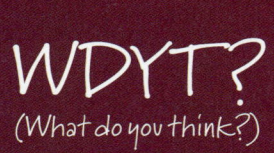

Could you unplug for a day, a week, a month or even longer?

TASK: Plan an Unplugging Day for your school and present your leaflet proposal to your class.

Learning outcomes
1. I can plan an Unplugging Day and present my proposal to the class.
2. I can use appropriate grammar and vocabulary from the unit in my proposal.
3. I can use my critical thinking skills to build a powerful argument.

Graphic organiser → Project planner p121

1 🎥 Watch a video of two students presenting their proposal. What makes their event suitable for all types of people?

STEP 1: THINK

2 Look at the Model project. Which pieces of information 1–6 do you need to include in your leaflet proposal?
1. a title and headings
2. reasons for the event
3. date, time and location
4. the activities
5. entrance fee
6. signing up for the event

STEP 2: PLAN

3 Work in pairs. Brainstorm some ideas for your day. Think of a good title, the date and time and some possible activities.

4 Work in pairs. Read the tips in the Super skills box and practise saying the Key phrases with a partner.

CRITICAL THINKING

SUPER SKILLS

Building a powerful argument

Tips

Brainstorm a list of reasons why people should attend your event.

Keep your arguments simple and direct.

Remember, you may need to change someone's mind about something, so make sure you understand their point of view.

Key phrases

We've agreed on the event, so now we need to think about why people should attend.

Let's brainstorm a few ideas.

Do you think this argument is convincing/compelling/powerful enough?

I think we need to include more … if we're going to persuade people.

Good point!/You're right!

5 Read the *How to …* tips on p121. Then think of some reasons why your event shouldn't be missed.

STEP 3: CREATE

6 Create your leaflet proposal. Use the tips and Key phrases in the Super skills box.

7 Decide who's going to say each part and practise your proposal.

Grammar and Vocabulary → Quick review p93

Model project

NATIONAL UNPLUGGING DAY

WHAT?
Get a team together and take part in a day of challenges – why not try your hand at our obstacle course? For those who prefer something less energetic, compete for maximum points in our end-of-day quiz. Great prizes in all sorts of categories such as collaboration, creativity and the fastest team to answer the questions.

HOW?
Sign your team up for the event on the school website. There's no maximum number for the teams, but only three members can take part in each event. We also hope that each team member takes part in at least one event.

WHY?
Spend some 'quality fun' time with your friends. Lock up your devices and get up off the sofa. If you can walk to the event, even better!

WHEN AND WHERE?
17th June: from noon until late afternoon on the sports field.
If it rains, the event will be moved to the school gym.

HOW MUCH?
Free to all. However, if you are able to make a donation, we will give the money to a local children's charity.

TURN YOUR PHONES OFF AND HAVE SOME FUN!

STEP 4: PRESENT

8 Present your proposal to the class. Use your leaflet to help you.

9 **Peer review** Watch the presentations and think of one or two questions to ask each group. Which event(s) would you attend? Why?

7 FINAL REFLECTION

1 **The task**
   Were your classmates interested in your proposal?
   Was your leaflet clear?

2 **Super skill**
   Did you come up with some sound arguments for celebrating the day?

3 **Language**
   Did you use new language from this unit? Give examples.

Beyond the task
Research some other national days online for this month. Choose one of the days and think of reasons why it should be celebrated. Propose your idea to the class.

8 Make a difference

WDYT? (What do you think?)

How can you contribute to make society better?

Vocabulary: global issues; phrasal verbs for achieving goals

Grammar: verb patterns: gerunds and infinitives; *try* and *regret*; verb + object + (*not*) infinitive; *used to, be used to, get used to*

Reading: an article about emoji

Listening: a radio interview about success stories

Speaking: politely interrupting

Writing: a formal letter of complaint

Project: design an emoji and create a digital poster about it.

Video skills p97

Real-world speaking p103

Project pp106–107

Global issues

1. Copy and complete the table with the issues in the box. Can you add any more?

   cyber-bullying   deforestation   endangered species   extinction   identity theft   online fraud   phishing scam   pollution

Environment	Technology
deforestation	

2. Work in pairs. Which issue(s) do you think are the most/least serious? Why?

3. Look at icons 1–16. What goals do you think they refer to?

4. Work in pairs. Look at the icons. Which do you think are the five most effective designs? Why?

Vocabulary 8

6 Match the words in the box with definitions 1–7.

> discrimination   gender equality   inclusion
> infrastructure   responsible consumption
> sustainable   scarcity

1 designed to cause the least possible harm to the environment
2 a situation in which the rights and opportunities are the same for people of all genders
3 not enough of something
4 the belief that all people should feel they are included in society
5 unfair treatment of someone because of their race, religion or other personal features
6 sensible use of things such as energy or fuel
7 systems and services (e.g. transport, phone networks) within a place or organisation

7 🔊 50 Listen to Zane and Malia discussing photos A–C and answer the questions.

1 In what order do they discuss photos A–C?
2 How many young people are currently out of school?
3 How many coastal areas have improved over the last few years?
4 What percentage of the world's population will live in cities by 2030?

8 💬 Work in pairs. Ask and answer the questions.

1 Which issues are most important to you? Why?
2 Which issues affect young people more? Why?

5 🎯 Check the meaning and pronunciation of the words and phrases in the box. Then answer the questions.

> affordable clean energy   climate change
> conflict resolution   discrimination
> diversity and inclusion   food security
> gender equality   homelessness
> investment in infrastructure   justice
> lack of sanitation   literacy and numeracy
> no access to education   ocean conservation
> poverty   protecting biodiversity   racism
> refugees   responsible consumption
> right to vote   sustainable cities   tolerance
> unemployment   water scarcity

1 Which goal/goals 1–16 does each issue relate to?
2 Which are positive objectives? Which are issues to tackle?

VIDEO SKILLS

9 🎥 Watch the video. What does plogging involve?

10 💬 Work in pairs. After watching the video, do you think plogging is popular? Why/Why not?

8 Reading and critical thinking

An article

1 💬 Work in pairs. Draw as many different emoji as you can think of in one minute. Compare in pairs and answer the questions.
1 Did you draw any of the same emoji?
2 Which emoji do you never/rarely/sometimes/often use?
3 Do you ever use emoji to talk about global issues? How?

2 Look at the article title and photos. Which global issues do you think will be mentioned? Skim the article and check your guesses.

3 🔊 51 Read and listen to the article. Complete the sentences in your own words with ideas from the text.
1 People use more than ten billion …
2 The advantages of emoji are …
3 Many of Shigetaka Kurita's original emoji designs … those we use today.
4 Every 12 months, the Unicode Consortium usually …
5 The peace emoji was the idea …
6 In the future, people … only emoji.

▶ **Subskill: Summarising a text in your own words**

To summarise a text, you should identify the main idea and important arguments, and then express these using your own words. It is important to:
- convey the ideas clearly and concisely
- omit examples and extra details

4 Match summaries a–d with paragraphs 1–6. Which paragraphs do not match with a summary?

a Newer emoji are far more diverse and inclusive, and include things specific to different cultures around the world. There is now an emoji for wheelchair users.

b Emoji are used worldwide. They are easily recognisable and everyone can understand them – it doesn't matter what language you speak. People use them when writing things such as texts and social media posts.

c In the future, emoji may allow us to discuss issues and describe deeper feelings and ideas. A group is currently working on an emoji for forgiveness.

d Emoji are a quickly growing, attractive visual language. There were originally 176.

5 Read the summaries in exercise 4 again. Follow the steps in the Subskill to eliminate unnecessary information.

6 Read the article again. Choose the correct option to complete the sentences.
1 When we use emoji, our messages contain more **language/feelings**.
2 Shigetaka Kurita created the emoji to improve how people **understand/share** messages.
3 Unicode Consortium **manage and approve/design and select** every emoji to be released.
4 *Emojination* wants to help people create emoji that are more **diverse/sophisticated**.
5 Having cultural and traditional emoji makes it possible for people to choose **suitable/unsuitable** emoji.

7 Write a summary of paragraphs 3 and 6. Use the summaries in exercise 4 to help you.

8 **Word work** Match the definitions with the words in bold in the article.
1 plans or suggestions, especially formal ones, that a group has to consider
2 something that prevents people from communicating
3 deliberately aiming to involve all types of people
4 to include more variety
5 complicated and advanced in design
6 got ideas or help to develop something from a large number of people, usually members of the public using the internet

9 💬 Work in pairs. Answer the questions.
1 When and how often do you use emoji?
2 What's your favourite emoji? Why?

CRITICAL THINKING

1 **Remember** State why emoji are so popular.
2 **Analyse** Examine the advantages and disadvantages of using them. When would you not use them?
3 **Evaluate** Do you think students should use emoji in essays and other written work? Justify your answer.

EMOJI FOR ALL

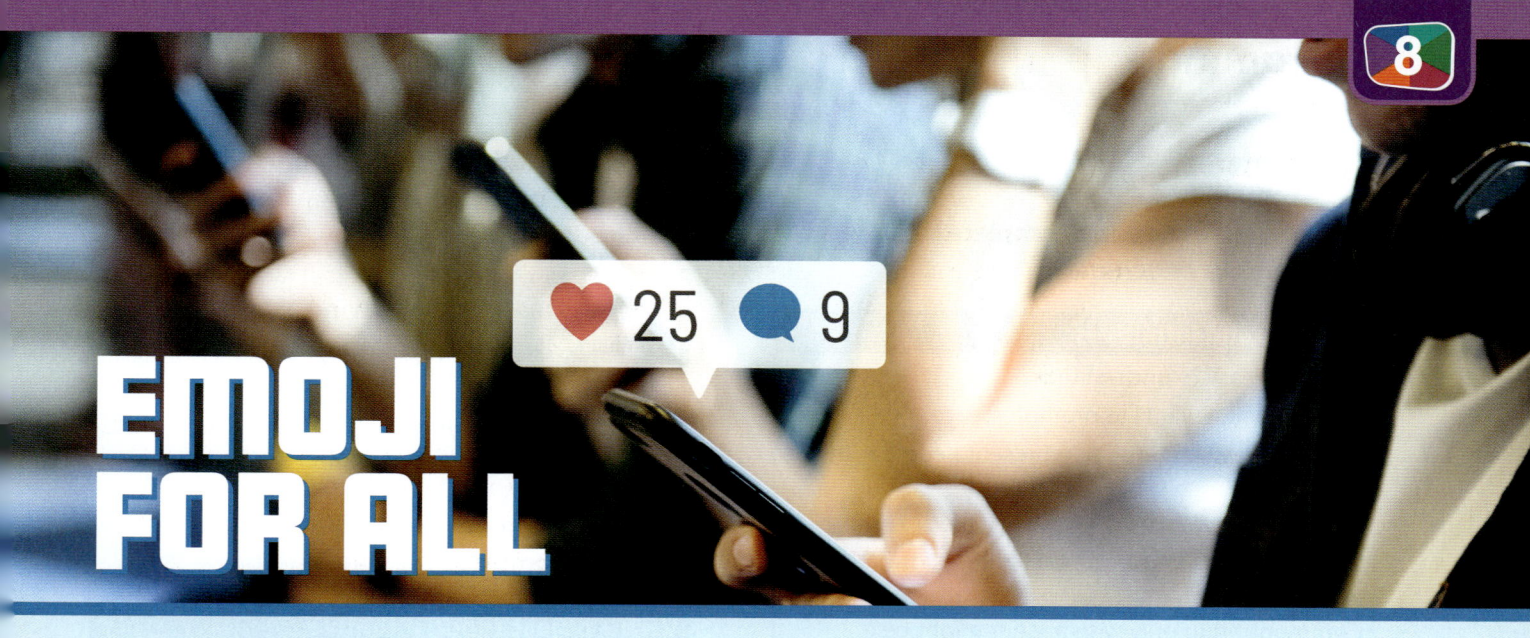

1. Do you speak emoji? Ninety-five per cent of internet users do! Most of us can't remember using an emoji for the first time, but it's hard to imagine life without them now. Over ten billion are sent every day and they're everywhere, from texts and social media to advertising and even official documents. These colourful images are more than just decoration: we use them to add tone and emotion to our messages. They are easy to understand, they cross language **barriers** and are popular worldwide.

2. Emoji began in Japan in 1999 and have come a long way since then. The word comes from the Japanese words *e* (picture) + *moji* (character). Shigetaka Kurita, an artist, created 176 of them as an instant and effective way of sharing information visually. They were a hit and people everywhere loved using them. That number has now increased to over 3,000 and grows every year. Today's emoji are far more stylish and **sophisticated** to look at, and some are almost unrecognisable from the originals.

3. So who creates new emoji? A non-profit organisation called the Unicode Consortium has managed and approved emoji since 2010, and they usually release all new emoji annually. Anyone can make a proposal, though the process can take up to two years. Imagine seeing your own emoji! If you're stuck for ideas, *Emojination*, which was co-founded by Yiying Lu, has plenty. It aims to **diversify** emoji even further by allowing people to collaborate on **proposals** and helping them work on their own ideas.

4. Emoji are evolving and reflect far greater gender equality, diversity and inclusion and cultural awareness than they ever have before. Now, you can change skin tones and hair colours on the human emoji, professions and sports show both males and females and there are also gender-neutral people. Recently, emoji were added to represent people with disabilities, including aids like wheelchairs, prosthetic limbs and guide dogs. There is an increasing variety of foods, traditional clothes, transport and animals – all from different countries.

5. What of the future? Will we get emoji to talk about more complex feelings? And what about global issues? Already, a group of organisations in Finland have **crowdsourced** an emoji for 'forgiveness' by asking people to send them designs for it. The #forgivemoji campaign wants to promote peace and give people a way to say 'sorry', and campaigners hope Unicode will approve the winning design.

6. Communicating using only emoji might be a dream for now, but it could happen. The fact that they are becoming more **inclusive** means they are increasingly a language where everyone is represented – a real global digital language of the future.

Did you know?

The food emoji that are used most often all year round are the birthday cake and pizza slice. The dumpling emoji is used in many different countries other than China – for example, Poland has *pierogi*, Spain and Argentina have *empanadas* and Russia has *pelmeni*.

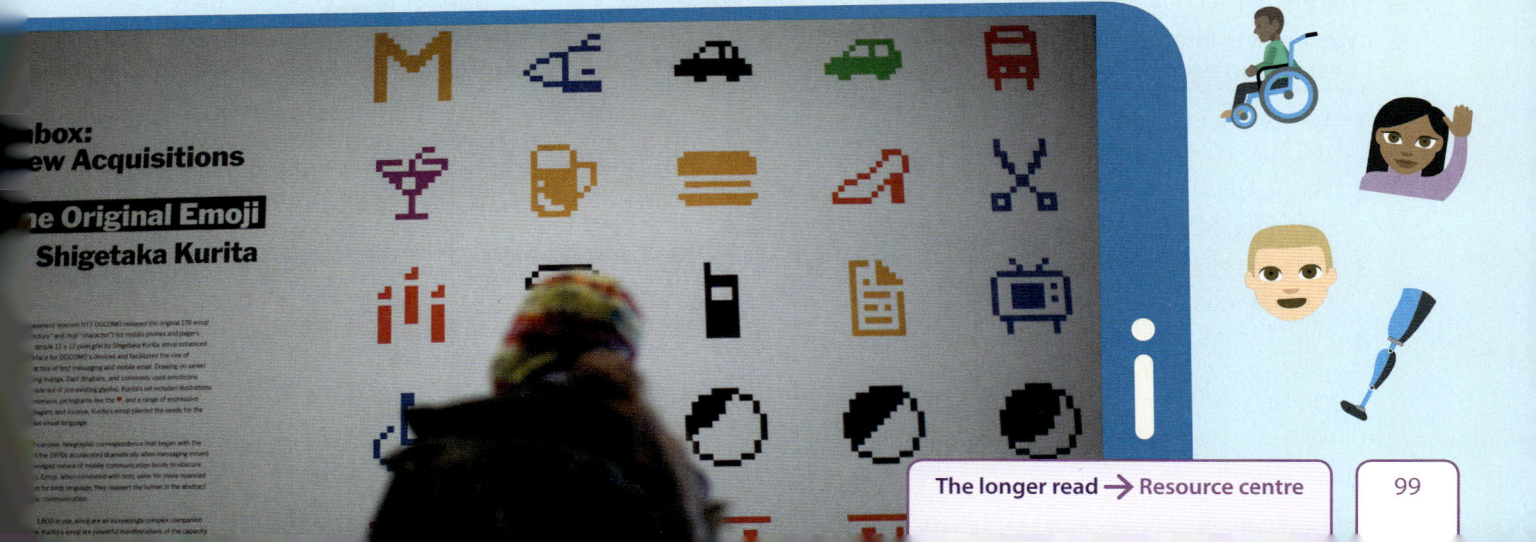

8 Grammar

Verb patterns

1 Read the examples and complete the rules with *infinitive* or *gerund*.

> **Gerunds and infinitives**
> Emoji are easy to understand.
> The campaign wants to promote peace.
> New emoji were added to represent people with disabilities.
> Imagine seeing an emoji you've created.
> Emoji are an effective way of sharing information visually.
> Communicating only with images might be a dream, but it could happen.

1. We use the (…) to express purpose, after certain verbs and after adjectives.
2. We use the (…) as the subject of a sentence, after certain verbs and after prepositions.

2 Complete the sentences with gerunds or infinitives.

1. Last week, I forgot (…) **(tidy)** my bedroom.
2. I've always wanted (…) **(travel)** around the world.
3. My best friend can't stand (…) **(get up)** early.
4. Last year, I stopped (…) **(eat)** meat.
5. In my opinion, it's important (…) **(listen)** carefully to people.
6. (…) **(use)** emoji helps me because I spend less time typing.
7. I used the emoji (…) **(show)** how sad I felt.

3 Work in pairs. Write questions for the sentences in exercise 2. Ask and answer.

4 Complete the rules with *gerund* or *infinitive*.

> **try, regret**
> They tried using different animal emoji.
> I've tried to design a new emoji, but I couldn't.
> I regret not sending my proposal. I wish I had!
> We regret to inform you that your proposal has been unsuccessful.

1. We use *try* + (…) to talk about something that was difficult or impossible to achieve.
2. We use *try* + (…) to talk about experimenting with something to see if it achieves the result you want.
3. We use *regret* + (…) to talk about something we wish we had/hadn't done in the past.
4. We use *regret* + (…) to give bad news formally: the meaning is similar to *be sorry to say*.

5 Choose the correct option.

1. I regret not **to study/studying** harder for my exams. It was a mistake.
2. We experimented with different face designs. We even tried **to have/having** green ones!
3. I tried **to explain/explaining** how to use emoji, but it didn't work.
4. I regret **to say/saying** that there will be no sports events this year. It's impossible.

6 Read the examples and choose the correct option to complete the rules.

> **Verb + object + (*not*) infinitive**
> It helps them to work on their own ideas.
> Do you expect us to believe you?
> The teacher encouraged the students not to work alone.

1. After some verbs (*invite*, *persuade*, *warn*, *remind*, etc.), we need an object + **gerund/infinitive**.
2. The object can be a noun or **pronoun/adjective**.

7 Write sentences with the correct form of the words in brackets.

1. Can you remind **(I / phone)** Sam later?
2. They advised **(we / not travel)** during the storm.
3. Sara is good at maths, so Dave wanted **(she / help)** him with his homework.
4. The teacher told **(they / not talk)** in class.

8 Correct the mistakes. One sentence is correct.

1. I'm delighted being here today.
2. He's finished designing a new emoji.
3. Katia is good at to listen to people.
4. I don't want that they tell Sam my secret.
5. Next week I mustn't forget handing in my project.
6. After to watching the video, we can have lunch.

9 Answer the question to solve the Brain teaser.

BRAIN TEASER

Max wanted to get his hair cut. He arrived in a village with only two hairdressers. After entering the first hairdresser's, he saw it was clean and tidy, and the hairdresser's hair was perfect. The second hairdresser's shop was a mess and his haircut was terrible.

Where did Max decide to get his hair cut? Why?

Vocabulary and Listening 8

Phrasal verbs for achieving goals

1 Read the advert. Who would you recommend? Why?

> **Never Give Up** is looking for people to appear in its new series. Do you know someone whose hard work **paid off**? Perhaps they've **started up** a company which has **taken off**, and they always manage to **work out** a solution for any problem. Or maybe they've launched a campaign which has **caught on** even though people said they would never **pull** it **off**. Or perhaps they **took over** from someone else because a campaign was failing. They set goals, never **put off** taking action, **stick to** their plans and **carry on** even when things are difficult. Maybe you have a friend who **sorts out** everyone's problems and isn't afraid to **take on** a global issue. We want to hear about them.
>
> Contact Beth Taylor at bethtaylor@radio7.com

2 Work in pairs. Choose the correct option. Then discuss if you agree with the statements.
1 When you make a plan, you should always **stick to/take on** it and not make changes.
2 It's easy to **take off/start up** a charity event.
3 When something goes wrong, the best thing is to **carry on/pull off**.
4 My best friend always helps me **take over/work out** what to do when I have a problem.
5 I'm happy when something I've worked hard at **pays off/sorts out** and I get good results.
6 I'm always ready to **take on/catch on** a new challenge.

Phrasal verbs with more than one meaning
Some phrasal verbs have more than one meaning, e.g. *take off, catch on, pull off, put off*.

3 Read the sentences and choose the best meaning for the phrasal verbs in bold.
1 remove/become successful
   a Her business has really **taken off**. It's really popular.
   b He **took off** his jacket because he was hot.
2 understand/become popular or fashionable
   a I wasn't sure at first, but then I **caught on**.
   b Sports drinks have really **caught on**. Everyone drinks them now.

A radio interview

4 🔊 52 Look at the photo. Read the text and answer the questions. Then listen and check.

19:40 SUCCESS STORIES

Tonight's episode features video game designer Lual Mayen, whose game about refugees has become an international hit.

1 Who is Lual Mayen?
2 Why do you think his video game might be unusual?

▶ **Subskill: Correcting mistakes**
Make sure you understand each part of the sentence and underline the key words. Listen and identify the relevant part of the interview, and note down the correct information. Then listen again and check your answers.

5 Listen again and correct the mistakes.
1 Silvia loves computer games and was amazed when she heard about Lual's game.
2 In the game, players are refugees who have to escape a war zone because there are no resources like water, food and medicine.
3 Lual was one of millions of people who had to leave Uganda due to a civil war.
4 Lual first saw a computer when he was 12 and his mum was given one three years later.
5 Over 26 million people voted online when Lual won the Global Gaming Citizen Award.

6 Answer the questions.
1 What does *Salaam* mean in Arabic?
2 What percentage of teens say they play video games?
3 How long did it take Lual to reach a place he could use his laptop?
4 What inspired him to create his video game?
5 What two things did Lual teach himself?
6 Why did he create the board game *Wahda*?

7 Work in pairs. Would you like to play *Salaam* or a similar video game? Why/Why not?

8 Grammar

used to, be used to, get used to

1 Read the examples and match 1–3 with a–c to make rules.

> Lual **used to live** in a refugee camp in Uganda.
> Where **did** Lual **use to live**?
> Most teens **are used to playing** video games.
> What **are** most teens **used to doing**?
> He **isn't getting used to living** in the USA. It's very different.
> Where **is** Lual **getting used to living**?

1 We use *used to* + bare infinitive …
2 We use *be used to* + gerund …
3 We use *get used to* + gerund …

a to talk about the process of becoming familiar with something.
b to talk about past habits and states.
c to talk about something we are accustomed to doing.

2 Choose the correct option.
1 I'm used to **speak/speaking** English in class. We usually do it.
2 My friend used to **live/living** in a different town.
3 When I was younger, I wasn't used to **learn/learning** a foreign language, but now I am.
4 I didn't use to **be/being** such a good swimmer, but I practised a lot.
5 When I started secondary school, I wasn't used to **be/being** with so many other students, but I've got used to **see/seeing** everyone now.

3 💬 Work in pairs. Write questions to find out if the sentences in exercise 2 are true or false for your partner. Then ask and answer.
1 *Are you used to speaking English in class?*

4 Read the sentences. Where do nouns and object pronouns go?

> **be used to/get used to + noun/pronoun**
> I lived in a village before, but I'm used to **the city** now.
> I found the buses hard to use at first, but I'm used to **them** now.
> Living in a flat is different, but I'm sure I'll get used to **it**.
> I'm getting used to **the traffic**.

5 Correct the mistakes. There is one correct sentence.
1 I didn't used to like going shopping, but now I often go at the weekend.
2 She used to living somewhere quiet before. She's not used to the noise here.
3 I never used to go to bed so late, but I've got used to do it now.
4 As a vegetarian, he's used to not eating meat, though he used to eat it every day.
5 These headphones felt strange when I first used them, but I've got used to they now.

6 Choose the correct option.

GRAMMAR ROUND-UP
1 2 3 4 5 6 7 8

SAVING THE WORLD

Amira Odeh Quiñones, **1 who/whose/whom** is from Puerto Rico, is a regional organiser for 350.org, an international climate organisation that campaigns for clean energy. Why does she think it's so important? Amira has seen the effects of climate change first-hand. She remembers **2 swim/swimming/to swim** in a coral reef as a child, but the reef **3 is being/has been/was** destroyed since then. In 2017, Puerto Rico **4 had suffered/suffered/has been suffering** from the effects of a terrible hurricane. **5 Seeing/Seen/To see** that devastation made her **6 almost/by far/significantly** more determined to act. Amira has recommended **7 focused/that people focus/to focus** on the needs of local communities. I admire Amira – if only more people **8 are/had been/were** like her! We **9 can/might/must** act now to build a better world. If we **10 didn't/don't/wouldn't**, then things will get worse.

Research
Find out about other young people who are campaigning for action on climate change. Where are they from? What are they doing?

Real-world speaking 8

Politely interrupting

1 🎥 Watch the video. Which charity do they decide to raise money for?

2 Watch again. Complete gaps 1–4 in the dialogue.

3 Watch again. Which Key phrases do you hear?

Gabby
Right, so we've got to plan a charity **1** (…). First, we should decide what charity we're fundraising for. I've got lots of ideas, so …

Lucy
Sorry to interrupt, but what if people want to raise money for different charities?

Gabby
Good point. I've got a **2** (…) here, so shall we see if there is one charity we all agree on?

Lucy
Maybe, but could I ask something? Why do we need just one charity? We could choose lots of different ones …

Jason
Sorry to **3** (…) you off, but raising money for lots of different charities might be hard. I did a sponsored race once …

Lucy
Well, hang on, I'll just finish what I have to say and then you can tell us about the race. As I was saying, we could raise money for different charities by having a charity fair.

Gabby
What's that? Do you mean an event with different stalls or activities?

Lucy
Yes, each stall or activity would raise money for a specific charity.

Jason
That's a **4** (…) idea!

4 Create your own dialogue. Follow the steps in the Skills boost.

SKILLS BOOST

THINK
You are discussing an issue with a friend and need to politely interrupt.

PREPARE
Prepare your dialogue. Remember to use some of the Key phrases.

PRACTISE
Practise your dialogue.

PERFORM
Act out your dialogue for the class or record it and play it to the class.

5 **Peer review** Listen to your classmates and answer the questions.
  1 Did they interrupt politely and respectfully?
  2 Which Key phrases did they use?

Key phrases

Politely interrupting
Sorry to interrupt, but …
Do you mind if I/Could I just add/ask something?
If I could interrupt for a moment?
Before you go on, I'd like to say something …
Sorry to cut you off, but …

Continuing to speak
Sorry, but I haven't finished yet./Wait a minute …/
As I was saying, …
I'll just finish what I have to say …

Real-world grammar

What if people want to raise money for different charities?
Raising money for lots of different charities might be hard.

Phrasebook → p125 Pronunciation: Intonation when interrupting → p117

8 Writing

Sea Green YOUTH CENTRE

12 Whitegate Street
L23 1GG
Tel: 07154 876534
i.gates05@mail.com

Councillor Logan
Winton Green Council
Liverpool L23 5FR

19th June 2021

Dear Mr Logan,

A **I am writing to express my concern** at the news that Sea Green Youth Centre is likely to be closed due to proposed cuts in funding.

B I have no doubt that the centre is a valuable resource for the community. It has been open for ten years, during which time it has provided a safe space for young people to take part in a range of leisure activities, learn new skills and meet other teenagers. Currently, the centre is regularly used by over 50 young people. In addition, it runs job opportunity courses and workshops which are designed to increase young people's chances of employment.

C I truly feel that closing the centre **is unacceptable** because there are very few local facilities for teenagers. Since it opened, youth crime and vandalism in the area have decreased. Furthermore, the centre has succeeded in helping hundreds of young people apply for and obtain jobs in an area of high unemployment. If the centre stopped doing activities and courses, I strongly believe that young people in the area would suffer.

D **I would be grateful if you could** look into the matter. **I trust that you will take steps to** ensure that funding is not cut. I am absolutely convinced that allowing this centre to carry on is essential for our community.

I look forward to your prompt response on this issue.

Yours sincerely,
Isabel Gates

A formal letter of complaint

1 Read the letter. What does Isabel want the result of her letter to be?

2 Match descriptions 1–4 with paragraphs A–D.
1 background information
2 what you would like to happen
3 the problem
4 reason for writing

3 Copy and complete the table with expressions from the letter.

Expressing strong opinions	Adding information
	In addition

▶ Subskill: Using formal language

In a letter of complaint, we use formal language to express what we want to say, e.g. *I must insist that, I look forward to your prompt response, This is unacceptable.*

4 Read the letter again. Match definitions 1–5 with the phrases in bold in the letter.

Which phrase is used to … ?
1 say something is wrong or not allowable
2 politely say what you expect someone to do
3 politely say you would like them to respond quickly
4 explain why you are writing and say you are unhappy about something
5 politely thank someone in advance for doing something

104

5 Rewrite the sentences with the passive to make them more formal. Where appropriate, use phrases to express strong opinions.

1 I think the council should create cycle lanes in the city centre.
2 The council is going to build more roads. I think everyone would benefit if they all had cycle lanes.
3 I really think people would use the cycle lanes.
4 More people used cars last year. I think this is because it is currently not safe to cycle.
5 The council are not repairing roads quickly. I think this makes them dangerous for cyclists.

6 Write a letter of complaint to your local council about a problem. Follow the steps in the Skills boost.

SKILLS BOOST

THINK
Think of a current issue where you live that you would like the council to act on. Use one of the ideas below or your own idea.
- the local park is full of litter
- there are plans to close your local sports centre
- the roads near schools are always very busy

PREPARE
Make notes for your letter to the council. Organise your notes into four paragraphs. Use the paragraph plan in exercise 2 to help you.

WRITE
Write your letter. Use the Model letter and the notes above to help you.

CHECK
Read your letter and answer the questions.
1 Have you used grammar and vocabulary from the unit?
2 Have you organised your letter correctly?
3 Have you used passives and expressions for giving strong opinions?
4 Have you used formal expressions for making complaints?

7 **Peer review** Exchange your letter with another student. Answer the questions.
1 Has the writer explained the background and expressed the problem clearly?
2 Has the writer said what they would like to happen?
3 Does the letter make you want to take action about this problem? Give reasons for your answer.

QUICK REVIEW 8

Grammar

Verb patterns

Gerunds and infinitives
We use the gerund and infinitive in different ways.
Dropping litter is a serious problem.
I am interested in **reducing** litter in the area.
We need more litter bins **to stop** people throwing rubbish in the street.
It's important **to understand** the problem.
Why has the council decided **not to install** any bins?
After some verbs, we can use either the gerund or infinitive with little or no change of meaning:
begin   can't stand   continue   hate   like   love   prefer   start
After these verbs there is a change of meaning depending on whether we use the gerund or infinitive:
forget   regret   remember   stop   try

Verb + object + (not) infinitive
We use the verb + object + infinitive with certain verbs. The object can be a noun or object pronoun.
They invited **us to write** a proposal for more bins.
We need to encourage people **not to drop** litter.
They instructed us **not to throw out** so much rubbish.

used to, be used to, get used to
We use *used to* + infinitive to talk about past habits/states, *be used to* + gerund/noun/pronoun to talk about being accustomed to something and *get used to* + gerund/noun/pronoun to talk about the process of becoming accustomed to something.
The park **used to be** clean, but now there's lots of litter.
I'**m used to** playing sports outside – I rarely play inside.
If you install more bins, people **will get used to** using them.

Vocabulary

🔊 53 Issues
cyber-bullying, deforestation, endangered species, extinction, identity theft, online fraud, phishing scam, pollution

🔊 54 Global issues
affordable clean energy, climate change, conflict resolution, discrimination, diversity and inclusion, food security, gender equality, homelessness, investment in infrastructure, justice, lack of sanitation, literacy and numeracy, no access to education, ocean conservation, poverty, protecting biodiversity, racism, refugees, responsible consumption, right to vote, sustainable cities, tolerance, unemployment, water scarcity

🔊 55 Phrasal verbs for achieving goals
carry on, catch on, pay off, pull off, put off, sort out, start up, stick to, take off, take on, take over, work out

105

8 Project

WDYT? (What do you think?)

How can you contribute to make society better?

TASK: Design a new emoji and create a digital poster to justify the need for it.

Learning outcomes
1 I can design an emoji and create a digital poster with relevant information.
2 I can use appropriate grammar and vocabulary from the unit in my poster.
3 I can use collaboration skills to show respect for others and consider diversity and inclusion.

Graphic organiser → Project planner p121

1 Watch the video of a group of students presenting their digital poster. What is their emoji for?

STEP 1: THINK

2 Look at the poster. Check the meaning of the words in bold and answer the questions.
   1 Who is the **target viewer** of the poster?
   2 What is the **main message** of the poster?
   3 Is the **layout** clear?
   4 Are the **images** effective?
   5 Are the **text fonts** and **styles** clear and effective?
   6 Is the emoji **design** effective?

STEP 2: PLAN

3 Work in pairs. Read the tips in the Super skills box and practise saying the Key phrases with a partner.

COLLABORATION — SUPER SKILLS

Respecting others

Tips

Think about your opinions before you speak. Could someone feel upset after working with you?

Think about people of different cultures, age groups, genders and backgrounds – is your emoji suitable for them?

Avoid stereotypes – do you need to find out more information?

Key phrases

That's true. / That's a good point – let's rethink (our idea).

That's only one way of looking at it … Should we consider … ?

I'm not sure I go along with that view …

That's not necessarily the case (because) …

We should look at this from a different perspective.

4 Work in groups. Decide what kind of emoji you want to create. Choose from the ideas or use your own idea.
- food and drink
- diversity and inclusion
- technology
- global issues
- feelings and emotions
- the environment
- smileys and people
- activities and sports

5 Discuss what the emoji should represent and look like. Use the tips and Key phrases in the Super skills box. Do any necessary research and make notes.

STEP 3: CREATE

6 In your groups, think about the questions in exercise 2 for your own poster. Read the *How to …* tips on p121 and write the text for the poster.

7 Create your emoji and your digital poster.

Model project

AN EMOJI FOR THIS PLANET

USES FOR THIS EMOJI
We don't have an icon to represent environmental issues yet.
- To tell friends about a cool eco-friendly product
- To show that something is good for the environment
- To recommend an environmental blog or website that is taking off
- To share some news about an environmental organisation that has just been set up

MEANING OF THIS EMOJI
The two green leaves:
- show the natural world.
- represent the environment.
- are a symbol of a healthy world.

The branch in the shape of a tick:
- points out that something is approved.

Together, they show that something is eco-friendly.

ADVANTAGES OF THIS EMOJI
- It is flexible and can be used in many situations.
- It is clear and easy to recognise.
- It is inclusive of everyone worldwide.
- It can be easily adapted for other environmental messages.

STEP 4: PRESENT

8 Practise presenting your digital poster in your groups.

9 Give your presentation to the class.

10 **Peer review** Listen to the other presentations or look at the digital posters and answer the questions.
1. Which posters do you like best? Why?
2. Which of the emoji would you use? Why?

8 FINAL REFLECTION

1 The task
Was your digital poster organised?
Was the design process successful?

2 Super skill
Did you collaborate well and respect others? Give examples.

3 Language
Did you use any new language from this unit? Give examples.

Beyond the task
Do you think we will ever communicate only with emoji? What would be the advantages and disadvantages of this? Are there times when it is better to use text?

107

9 Look what you know!

1. a t(...) e (...) d an e (...)(...) n t
2. s(...)t obj(...)c(...)(...)v(...)s
3. d i v e(...) s(...)(...) y and i n(...) l(...) s(...)(...)(...)
4. s u(...) p(...)(...) t(...) v e
5. t(...)(...) e i t (...) a (...) y
6. v o l c(...)(...) i (...) er(...) p(...)(...) o (...)
7. c(...)(...)(...) r ex(...)(...) t(...) d(...) y
8. a m a j(...)(...) br(...)(...) k-th(...) o u(...)(...)

Vocabulary

1 Complete the words to form the phrases represented in the photos.

2 Match vocabulary sets a–h with answers 1–8 from exercise 1.
   a Describing personality characteristics (Unit 1)
   b Innovation (Unit 2)
   c Social influencers (Unit 3)
   d Natural world (Unit 4)
   e Ways of talking (Unit 5)
   f Challenges (Unit 6)
   g Chilling out, getting active (Unit 7)
   h Global issues (Unit 8)

3 Which word or expression does not belong in each group? Why?
   1 research, challenge, progress, investigate
   2 make an effort, make up, make a mistake, make fun of
   3 overcooked, bilingual, distance, mistranslated
   4 come up with, get away with, do away with, take up
   5 start up, take on, become, pull off
   6 get over, get married, get ready, get better
   7 popular, citizenship, creativity, growth
   8 judge, rehearsal, broadcast, landslide

4 Add at least three more words to each group in exercise 3. Which unit are they from?

5 Choose the correct option a–c to complete the text.

Danielle Fisher

Danielle Fisher definitely likes a **1** (…). By the time she was just 20 years old, she'd become the youngest American to climb the Seven Summits (the tallest mountains on each of the seven continents, which includes Mount Everest). It wasn't easy, as Danielle also has ADD, which means she finds it hard to **2** (…) tasks without losing focus. But she is also very **3** (…) and once she'd decided to do it, there was no stopping her. It was difficult to **4** (…) as it involved a considerable amount of hard training – in the end, it took her two and a half years. Standing at the top of Everest, her final climb, must have been **5** (…) as the views are stunning. All of Danielle's hard work helped with her studies, too – climbing mountains meant she got **6** (…) at focusing. Her actions also **7** (…) other people her age. Although her record has since been beaten, what Danielle did shows that achieving a **8** (…) is possible if you have the motivation.

1	a challenge	b demand		c surprise
2	a go on about	b live up to		c get on with
3	a aggressive	b selfish		c determined
4	a catch on	b pull off		c sort out
5	a breakthrough	b mind-blowing		c unexpected
6	a care	b better		c ready
7	a resolved	b inspired		c achieved
8	a setback	b resolution		c goal

108

Look what you know! 9

Reading

1 Look back at the Reading subskills in Units 1–8. Which do you find the most useful? Why?

2 Look at the photos and headlines. Match topics 1–4 with headlines A–D. Then read the texts quickly and check your answers.
1 benefits of a positive feeling
2 young people tackling a global issue
3 popular challenges on the internet for people to try
4 something that might be built in the future

3 🔊 56 Read and listen to the texts again. Are the sentences true or false? Correct the false sentences.
1 There are around 100 species of lemur that are unique to Madagascar.
2 The Youth for Lemurs project is working with teenagers in all Madagascan villages.
3 Gratitude has a stronger effect on physical health than on relationships.
4 Feeling thankful helped improve people's immune systems.
5 3D printed houses could help solve more than one global issue.
6 The Italian architects' design was based on the construction of energy-efficient houses.
7 Neither the mannequin challenge nor the egg-balancing test were popular.
8 Adele took part in the mannequin challenge and the egg-balancing test.

4 **Word work** The words in bold in the texts appeared in the Word work exercises in Units 1–8. What part of speech are they and what do they mean?

5 Write a one-sentence summary of each text A–D.

6 💬 Work in pairs. Order the articles from most to least interesting. Compare with a partner and give reasons for your answers.

INTERESTING NEWS

A Teens saving wildlife

Most of Madagascar used to be covered in rainforest filled with millions of species of plants and animals. Today, due to intensive farming, it now holds the global record for deforestation. Teenage volunteers in ten villages are taking action to stop this **excessive** trend and to protect about 100 different types of lemur on the island. These species only live on Madagascar and are in danger of **extinction**. Working with a project called 'Youth for Lemurs', they are learning to farm without destroying the rainforest – and they will then be able to pass on their new skills so others can farm sustainably, too.

B Gratitude

Gratitude – that feeling of being thankful – has a positive effect on everything, from our relationships to our physical and mental health. In studies of over 1,000 people, those that regularly practised gratitude slept better, exercised more and it even **boosted** their immune systems. Additionally, they felt more optimistic, happier and more alert. When it came to relationships, they were more outgoing, helpful and understanding. They said they experienced less loneliness and were able to forgive others more easily.

C Print your house

Homelessness is a huge problem worldwide. Added to that, it is predicted that by 2030, five billion people will live in cities. However, climate change is also a growing concern. So, could an exciting **proposal** for 3D printed houses be the answer to all these issues? New sustainable houses, designed by Italian architects, will be built out of local soil and are both energy-efficient and resilient. The houses can be connected to form communities. The **spectacular** curved design was inspired by the way in which wasps construct their nests.

3D printed house by WASP

D Online challenges

People love sharing their videos and photos of the online challenges they take part in, but these trends are usually **short lived**. Two viral ones were the mannequin challenge and the egg-balancing test. The first involved doing a funny 'frozen' action pose – even celebrities like singer Adele and footballer Jamie Vardy got in on the act. The second was **straightforward**, but tricky to do: participants had to balance an egg on its tip during a solar eclipse. Impossible? Dozens of videos of eggs balanced on different surfaces showed it was achievable. Although most challenges are harmless fun, you definitely shouldn't go in for any dangerous ones.

9 Look what you know!

Grammar
Units 1 and 2

1 Choose the correct option.
1. They **have released/have been releasing/had released** a new song recently.
2. I had to walk into town because the bus **left/had left/had been leaving**.
3. Once, I **was going/went/had gone** on holiday to France with my friends.
4. I **didn't wear/wasn't wearing/haven't worn** my school uniform at 7:00 am this morning.
5. He **wasn't wearing/hasn't been wearing/didn't use to wear** colourful clothes when he was younger, but now he does.

2 Complete the dialogue with the correct past simple, past perfect or past perfect continuous form of the verbs in brackets. Use the continuous form where possible.

Sorry I **1** (…) **(not reply)** last night, but I **2** (…) **(be)** exhausted.

Why **3** (…) **(you be)** so tired last night?

Because Sam and I **4** (…) **(exercise)** for over an hour in the park!

We **5** (…) **(finish)** watching a documentary earlier about how good exercise is for you and we **6** (…) **(decide)** to get fit.

How **7** (…) **(you feel)** this morning?

Great! We **8** (…) **(never do)** anything like it before yesterday, but we're going to carry on.

3 Complete the sentences with future forms so they are true for you.
1. Next year, I hope I (…) .
2. At this time tomorrow, I (…) .
3. I'm (…) later.
4. I've made plans and next week I'm going to (…) .
5. By this time next week, I (…) .
6. Tomorrow, my last class (…) .

Units 3 and 4

1 Complete the text with the correct relative pronouns. Omit the pronoun where possible.

Andy Warhol, the famous artist and filmmaker **1** (…) works are famous worldwide, was born in Pennsylvania, USA, in 1928. In 1949, he moved to New York City **2** (…) he worked in advertising and for fashion magazines. It was perhaps this **3** (…) inspired him to create experimental artworks using images from popular culture, such as soda bottles and soup cans, in the early 1960s. This new style of art, **4** (…) was called 'Pop Art', became his trademark. The early 1960s was also the time **5** (…) he started painting portraits of famous people and set up his studio, **6** (…) became a meeting place for young artists, musicians and actors. Over the next few decades, Warhol had many exhibitions in many countries **7** (…) were a huge success. Warhol also experimented with his personal style and painted many self-portraits. These are pictures **8** (…) some people think are among his best.

2 Correct the mistakes in the sentences.
1. Sam could have gone out, that's impossible – he's in his bedroom.
2. You don't have to do it. It isn't permitted.
3. Playing a musical instrument is so interesting as learning a language.
4. My advice is that you can tell someone where you're planning to walk in case you get lost.
5. Having good friends is more important that having lots of money.
6. I spend little time at home than I used to; I was often at home before.
7. The exam was hard, but we could pass it because we'd studied a lot.
8. It might not have been easy to decide what to do – it was an impossible choice.

3 Complete the sentences with perfect modals.
1. It was a bad idea to do that. You (…) **(do)** it!
2. The robbers were so fast, the police (…) **(catch)** them even if they'd arrived sooner.
3. What a shame you had to miss the party. You (…) **(enjoy)** it!
4. Sam didn't try very hard – he's a great tennis player. He (…) **(win)** the match.
5. Why didn't you do the homework? You (…) **(do)** it.

Look what you know! 9

Units 5 and 6

1 Rewrite the sentences in reported speech. Make any necessary changes.

1 'Why didn't you go to the cinema yesterday?' he said to Sara.
   He asked (…) .
2 'It's raining here now', he said to me.
   He told (…) .
3 'I must leave immediately', Max said to us.
   He insisted (…) .
4 'Is it easy to write computer code?' she wondered.
   She wondered (…) .
5 'I'll text you tonight', she said to me.
   She promised (…) .
6 'Where will you meet us?' they said to him.
   They asked (…) .

2 Write the sentences in reported speech with the correct form of the verbs in brackets.

1 'Don't touch this book', he said to me. **(tell)**
2 'I'm sorry I did it', I said. **(apologise)**
3 'Readers should send funny stories to the show', they said. **(invite)**
4 'Would you mind not eating in here?' she said to us. **(ask)**
5 'We'll help you', they said to me. **(agree)**
6 'I didn't eat the chocolate', she said. **(deny)**
7 'I'll pay for the pizzas', he said. **(insist)**
8 'I saw Justin Bieber at the airport', he said to his sister. **(convince)**

3 Write full questions with the words given. Then answer the questions.

1 you / wish / you / can / drive?
2 if / you / have / a million euros / what / you / buy?
3 you / prefer / stay in / unless / your friends / invite you out?
4 you / wish / your friends / not text / you / so often?
5 who / you / like / to be / if / you / be born / in the past?
6 when / you / have a rival / it / increase / your motivation?

Units 7 and 8

1 Complete the text with the correct passive form of the verbs in brackets.

1 (…) **(it say)** that performing live and 'unplugged' is the true test of musicianship. That's the idea behind *MTV Unplugged*, an American TV show that **2** (…) **(first / broadcast)** in 1989. On the show, musicians play without electricity, for example, with an acoustic guitar or traditional piano, though microphones **3** (…) **(use)** and each performance **4** (…) **(record)** with a live audience. Although some shows **5** (…) **(record)** in TV studios, others have been concerts played in cities around the world. For one episode, a ship **6** (…) **(even / use)** in Hamburg Harbour. Alicia Keys gave one of the most memorable performances: while it **7** (…) **(film)**, several guest stars including Damian Marley delighted the audience with surprise appearances. Some programmes **8** (…) **(could / only / see)** online, though most were on TV. Acoustic albums **9** (…) **(release)** by many famous artists after they have appeared on the show. An episode **10** (…) **(show)** on TV later this evening – definitely one to watch!

2 Rewrite the sentences with the correct form of *have something done*.

1 A hairdresser is going to cut my hair later.
   I (…) .
2 Last year, decorators painted our house.
   We (…) .
3 They will deliver pizza to Mark tonight.
   Mark (…) .
4 The gardener is cutting the grass for me now.
   I (…) .
5 The beautician was painting Julia's nails when Sam phoned.
   Julia (…) .
6 They have repaired our car.
   We (…) .

3 Complete the sentences with the correct form of the verbs in brackets. Which ones are true for you?

1 I've decided (…) **(take up)** a new sport.
2 I'm used to (…) **(do)** lots of homework every day.
3 I can remember (…) **(learn)** to swim. It was fun!
4 I don't think it's important (…) **(exercise)** for a long time, as long as you do it regularly.
5 (…) **(play)** tennis is one of my favourite hobbies.
6 I mustn't forget (…) **(buy)** bread when I next go to the shops.
7 I think everyone should try (…) **(spend)** more time unplugged. It's good for you.

111

9 Look what you know!

Listening

1 Look back at the Listening subskills in Units 1–8. Which do you find most useful? Why?

2 Look at the photos and answer the questions.
1. What do you think each news story is about?
2. What words and phrases do you think you will hear?

3 🔊 57 Listen to the news stories and match the photos A–D with extracts 1–4. Were your guesses in exercise 2 correct?

4 Listen again and complete the sentences.
1. At first, Dan found (…) at the camp a challenge.
2. His friend Kaspar sends around (…) every day.
3. Different (…) have adopted Dr. Martens as a part of their identity.
4. The original Dr. Martens boot was called the (…) and came out in (…).
5. Only nine of the top 100 highest-earning movies were (…).
6. When the film director is female, there is a (…) in the number of female characters.
7. *Green News* has two stories about planting things to help with (…).
8. Seagrass Ocean Rescue are planting (…) seagrass seeds off the coast of West Wales.

5 🔊 58 Read the questions and underline the key words. Then listen to the rest of the news story and choose the correct option a–c.
1. Seagrass Ocean Rescue …
   a. was started up by Swansea University.
   b. hope to plant 20,000 m² of seagrasses.
   c. is looking for experienced biologists.
2. Which statement is true about seagrass?
   a. In 100 years' time, 92% of seagrass will have disappeared from UK coastal waters.
   b. More seagrass is destroyed by pollution than by boats or coastal development.
   c. Seagrass can take in carbon more quickly than tropical rainforests.
3. Shelby Barber …
   a. has planted a million trees in the UK.
   b. has already achieved her tree-planting goal.
   c. has come to the UK to plant trees.
4. At the moment, forests in the UK absorb around (…) tonnes of carbon dioxide.
   a. ten million
   b. 20 million
   c. 30 million
5. Shelby …
   a. doesn't earn much money for planting trees, although she's skilled.
   b. can plant up to 4,000 trees a day.
   c. only works a few hours each day because it's such hard work.

6 💬 Work in pairs. Answer the questions.
1. Which story did you think was most/least interesting? Why?
2. Which story surprised you most?

Look what you know! 9

Real-world speaking

1 **Match 1–6 with A–F. What phrases do you remember for each situation?**
   1 organising an event
   2 giving directions
   3 dealing with shopping issues
   4 politely interrupting
   5 checking understanding and clarifying
   6 discussing opinions

2 **Match questions 1–6 with responses a–f.**
   1 What if someone tells her before I see her?
   2 Can I ask why you're returning it?
   3 Do you get what I'm saying?
   4 Do you mind if I add something?
   5 Can't we book a different venue?
   6 Sorry to bother you, but we're looking for the sports centre.

   a Well, if I understand you correctly, we have to do it like this.
   b I'm afraid I can't help you. I'm not from round here.
   c You've got a point there. Phone her!
   d It doesn't fit properly.
   e Sorry, but I haven't finished yet.
   f Like where? What's wrong with the place we usually use?

3 **Work in pairs. Act out a short dialogue with the phrases in the box.**

   > How can I help you today?
   > You can exchange it for another one.
   > I'd like a refund please.

4 **Create your own dialogue. Follow the steps in the Skills boost.**

   ### SKILLS BOOST

   THINK
   Choose a situation and make notes.
   - You and a friend want to organise a surprise party for a student who is leaving school. Make suggestions, negotiate and agree on how to do it.
   - You are visiting a new city and need directions to the museum. Ask for directions, politely interrupt and ask for clarification where necessary.

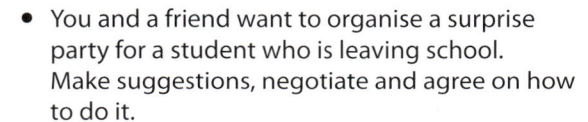

   PREPARE
   Prepare a dialogue. Remember to include relevant Key phrases.

   PRACTISE
   Practise your dialogue.

   PERFORM
   Act out your dialogue for the class or record it and play it to the class.

5 **Peer review** Listen to your classmates and answer the questions.
   1 Which task did they do? What did/didn't they do well?
   2 Which Key phrases did they use?
   3 Could they improve their dialogue? How?

9 Look what you know!

Writing

1 Read texts 1–8 quickly, then match them with text types a–h. Which unit was each text type in?

a A product review
b An informal article for a school magazine
c A description of a person
d A for-and-against essay
e A description of a place
f A formal letter of complaint
g An opinion essay
h A report

① Secondly, my personal view is that having celebrity role models is a good thing. Celebrities can use their fame to spread positive messages.

② I am writing to express my disappointment at the news that our local skate park is likely to be closed. I truly feel that the skate park is a great asset.

③ News   Destinations   Things to do   Hotels
The old town in Amsterdam is a charming place. You'll find plenty of shops with traditional crafts and restaurants serving delicious local cuisine.

④ What's new   Reviews   Top Tech   Search
★★★★☆
What I love about this tablet is that it's extremely easy to use. Despite being very light, it is well made.

⑤ Matt is quite tall with very short blond hair and blue eyes. He's extremely generous and absolutely hilarious.

⑥ On the one hand, video calls are a powerful tool which can be used in many different ways – from staying in touch with family to distance learning. Furthermore, they can be used for business purposes.

⑦ **CONTENT**
Most people agreed that:
- the content was well thought-out
- the contents page was welcoming and clear

⑧ **Do you fancy the challenge of learning a new language?**
Here's your chance! Read our grammar tips and learn about another culture.

2 Find the words or features in the texts and answer the questions.

1 *despite*: What part of speech are *despite*, *in spite of*, *although*, *even though*? (Unit 2)
2 addressing the reader: What other features of an informal article can you remember? (Unit 6)
3 *I truly feel that*: What other expressions do you know for giving strong opinions? (Unit 8)
4 *Secondly*: What other words and phrases do you know to help organise your essay? (Unit 3)
5 *On the one hand*: What other expressions do you know for for-and-against essays? (Unit 7)
6 no article before a city: When else do we use no article? (Unit 4)
7 four adverbs: What other adverbs like *very* do you know? (Unit 1)
8 an expression to present key findings. What other expressions for writing reports are there? (Unit 5)

3 Choose a task and write your answer.

Task A 'We are too used to bad news. More good news should be reported.' Write an opinion essay.

Task B You want to encourage young people to spend more time 'unplugged'. Write an informal article about it for your school magazine.

SKILLS BOOST

THINK
1 Decide which task to do and make notes.
2 Find useful language from the book.

PREPARE
1 Organise your writing.
2 Think about the format of your text. Look back at the Model writing texts to help you.

WRITE
Write your opinion essay or informal article.

CHECK
Read your writing.
1 Did you use correct grammar, spelling and punctuation?
2 Did you use a range of vocabulary and appropriate connectors and phrases?

4 **Peer review** Exchange your writing with another student. Answer the questions.
1 Which task did your partner do?
2 Are the grammar, vocabulary, spelling and punctuation correct?

REVIEW GAME

Look what you know! 9

1 What is unusual about the companies adidas and PUMA?

2 Which two food emoji are used most often all year round?

3 When and why did Ella London start wearing yellow clothes?

4 Apart from the people who live on La Gomera, how many other groups of people use a whistling language?
a around 50
b over 70
c more than 90

5 This student won an award after inventing a new food preservation method. What is her name? Where is she from?

6 Where are Victoria Falls and how wide are they?

7 What did Lyle Zapato create as a hoax?
a The River Shark
b The Mountain Crab
c The Tree Octopus

8 Which US city does the competitive dance form 'breaking' come from?

9 What did Lual Mayen design and what was special about it?

10 Where is the Route of Parks and who created it?

11 Why did officials stop using facial recognition technology in Boston airport?

12 Dating from 79 CE, these things were found in the ruins of shops in Pompeii. You might see them on TV today. What are they?

13 What could these microdevices be used for in the future?

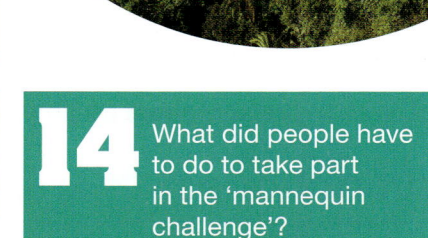

14 What did people have to do to take part in the 'mannequin challenge'?

15 When is Earth Hour celebrated?
a the first Saturday in May
b the second Saturday in July
c the last Saturday in March

16 What TV talent show is this? What do the contestants have to do?

Pronunciation

Unit 1
/h/

1. 🔊 59 **Listen to the sentences. Which /h/ sounds do we pronounce?**
   1. Harry has been wearing his horrible hat for hours.
   2. He hasn't done his history homework yet.
   3. He's travelled to Hungary wearing his historical clothes.

2. **Listen to the sentences again and repeat.**

Homophones

A homophone is a word that sounds the same as another word, but has its own spelling and meaning.

1. 🔊 60 **Listen to the pairs of words. Which are homophones?**
   1. whole   hole
   2. brake   break
   3. scene   seen
   4. price   praise
   5. threw   through
   6. receipt recipe

Unit 2
/æ/, /ɑː/ and /eɪ/

1. 🔊 61 **Listen and repeat the words.**

/æ/	/ɑː/	/eɪ/
adapt handy	advance fast	breakthrough embrace

2. 🔊 62 **Listen and repeat the words in the box. Do we pronounce the underlined sound /æ/, /ɑː/ or /eɪ/?**

b<u>a</u>dly-m<u>a</u>de   f<u>a</u>rm   h<u>a</u>rd-to-use   m<u>a</u>gnet
old-f<u>a</u>shioned   pr<u>a</u>ctical   r<u>a</u>ise   sh<u>a</u>rp rise

Intonation

1. 🔊 63 **Listen to the sentences. Is the speaker in each one excited or bored? Is there a rising or falling intonation?**
   1. I think you've missed the point here.
   2. A robot can discover illness through smelling our breath. What a breakthrough!
   3. AI can read our minds by understanding the signals from our brains. Mind-blowing!
   4. Here we go again. I don't have time for those kinds of people.

Unit 3
/b/ and /v/

1. 🔊 64 **Listen and repeat. Which word do you hear?**
   1. best   vest   3. berry   very
   2. ban   van   4. boat   vote

2. 🔊 65 **Now listen and repeat the sentences.**
   1. Celebrities deserve privacy at home, not visitors.
   2. She attended an event in a very small village to promote a band.

/ʃ/ and /tʃ/

1. 🔊 66 **Listen and repeat.**

/ʃ/	/tʃ/
<u>sh</u>ip	<u>ch</u>ip
relation<u>sh</u>ip	a<u>ch</u>ievement
satisfa<u>ct</u>ion	<u>ch</u>ampionship

2. 🔊 67 **Listen and repeat the words in the box. Do you hear /ʃ/ or /tʃ/?**

reader<u>sh</u>ip   relaxa<u>t</u>ion   close ma<u>tch</u>
resear<u>ch</u>   ri<u>ch</u> and famous   pre<u>ss</u>ure

Pronunciation

Unit 4
Word stress: nouns and verbs

> Where the same two-syllable word can be a noun or a verb, the stress is *often* on the **first** syllable of the noun and on the **second** syllable of the verb.

1 🔊 68 **Listen and repeat the words.**

Noun	Verb
1 **im**pact	im**pact**
2 **ob**ject	ob**ject**
3 **per**mit	per**mit**
4 **pro**gress	pro**gress**

2 🔊 69 **Look at the words in bold in the sentences. Which syllable is stressed? Listen and check.**

1. There's been an **increase**, not a **decrease**, in natural disaster films.
2. I **suspect** this trend isn't going to change.
3. They still need to **record** the soundtrack for the film.

Unit 5
Connected speech: word linking

1 🔊 70 **Listen to and repeat the expressions. Which sound at the end of the first word is linked to the beginning of the next word?**

first of all   What happened?

I apologised for it.   So did I!

2 🔊 71 **What sounds do you think are linked in the sentences? Listen, check and repeat.**

1. He suggested ordering a pizza.
2. That's unbelievable!
3. There must be loads of similar examples.
4. Please send in any more funny stories.

Unit 6
Sentence stress in conditionals

1 🔊 72 **Listen to the sentences. How many words do you hear in each one? (Contractions = two words.)**

2 **Listen again and write down the conditional sentences. Mark the stressed words.**

3 🔊 73 **Mark the stressed words in the sentences. Listen and check your answers.**

1. We'll go to the beach providing the weather's fine.
2. If I didn't live in this country, I'd live in Australia.
3. I'd have bought you a present if I'd known it was your birthday.

Unit 7
Word stress: expressions with *make* and *do*

1 🔊 74 **Listen and mark the stress in the sentences. Which part of the *make* and *do* collocation is stressed more?**

1. Make the most of the good weather while it lasts.
2. Please make up your mind! We need to go soon!
3. I'd love to do a degree in another country.

2 🔊 75 **Mark the stress in the sentences. Listen and check.**

1. Are you making fun of me?
2. I wish people would make more effort to clean up.
3. We need to make sure we're going the right way.

Unit 8
Intonation when interrupting

> When we interrupt someone, our voice starts high at the beginning of the expression and then goes down towards the end. If we're asking a *yes/no* question, our voice goes up again at the end of the question.

1 🔊 76 **Listen and repeat the sentences.**

1. Excuse me for a second, but that's not right.
2. Could I just ask something?

2 🔊 77 **Mark the intonation in the sentences. Listen, check and repeat.**

1. Is it OK if I jump in for a moment?
2. Sorry to cut you off, but I'd like to add something here.

Project planner

Unit 1 Graphic organiser

What makes you the person you are?
- clothes and colours
  - historical clothes
  - the colours of clothes you wear
- personality quizzes
- personal characteristics — determined, thoughtful …
- phrasal verbs — come up with, go in for …
- personal qualities — confident, reliable …

How to create a mind map
- Write your title in a box in the centre and draw branches out from the box.
- At the end of each branch, write a topic related to the main title in a circle. Then draw lines out from the circle.
- At the end of each line, write a key word, phrase or idea related to the topic or a further sub-topic.
- Continue expanding the mind map by adding further topics, sub-topics and key words or phrases.
- You can use different colours for each topic and images instead of words/phrases. Using bigger writing for the theme and topics and smaller writing for the key words/phrases can help.

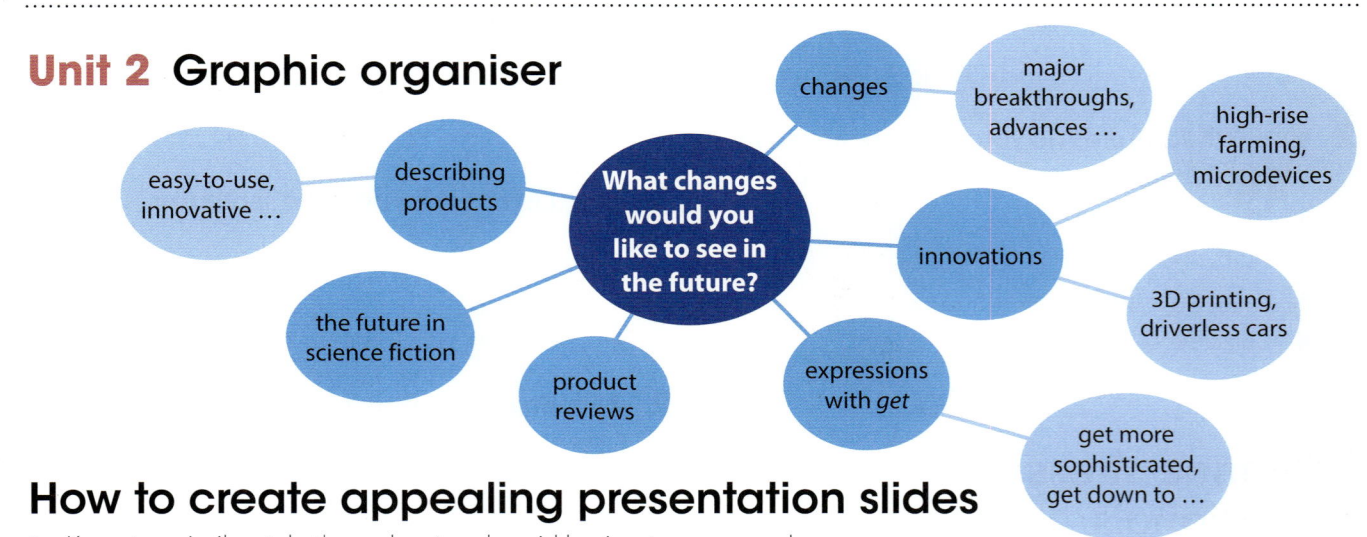

Unit 2 Graphic organiser

What changes would you like to see in the future?
- changes — major breakthroughs, advances …
- describing products — easy-to-use, innovative …
- the future in science fiction
- product reviews
- innovations — high-rise farming, microdevices; 3D printing, driverless cars
- expressions with *get* — get more sophisticated, get down to …

How to create appealing presentation slides
- Keep to a similar style throughout and avoid having too many colours.
- Choose a font and a font size which is easy to read, even from a distance.
- Use short, catchy titles or headings, and use one or two images to illustrate your ideas.
- Use bullet points and keywords. Avoid including too much text on each slide – you can expand on your points when you give the presentation.
- Check your slides for spelling and punctuation.

Project planner

Unit 3 Graphic organiser

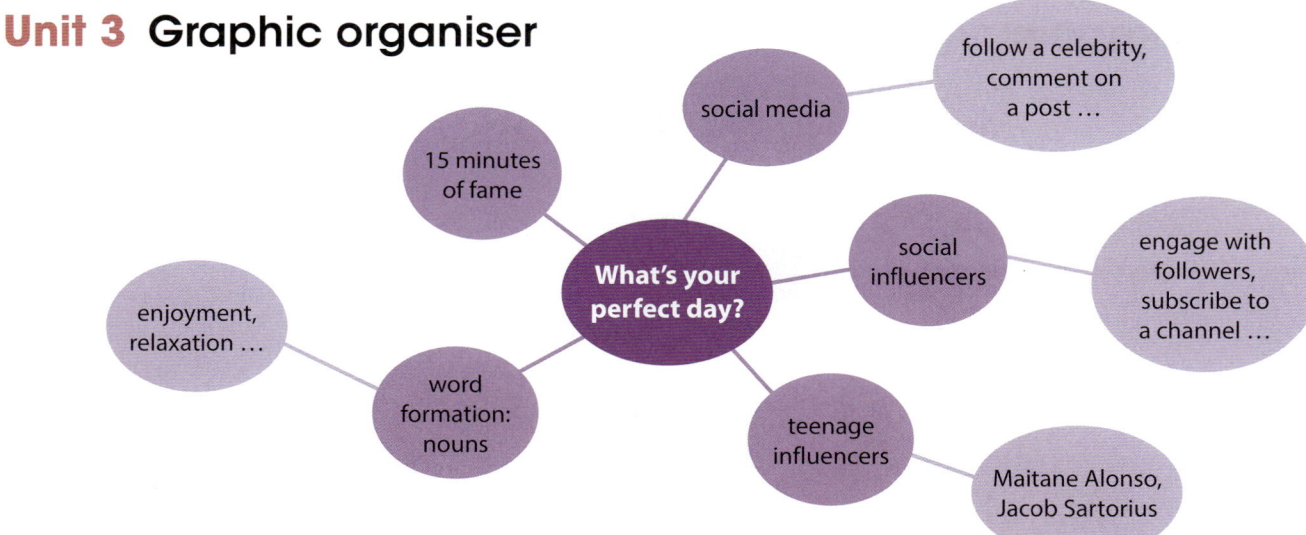

- What's your perfect day?
  - social media — follow a celebrity, comment on a post …
  - 15 minutes of fame
  - social influencers — engage with followers, subscribe to a channel …
  - teenage influencers — Maitane Alonso, Jacob Sartorius
  - word formation: nouns — enjoyment, relaxation …

How to make an effective video

- Plan your video in advance. Think about where your actors are going to be, when they're going to be there and what they're going to say.
- Shoot your video outside so you can use natural light. On a very sunny day, avoid shooting at midday when there are more shadows.
- Pay attention to the background. If there are too many people, buildings or objects behind the actors, this may be distracting for the viewer.
- Check your audio. Make sure your audience can hear what the actors are saying. If possible, use an external microphone.
- Keep your editing simple and add in one piece of music, not several.

Unit 4 Graphic organiser

- What is the best way to enjoy nature?
  - natural world
    - geographical features — canyon, coral reef …
    - natural disasters — avalanche, drought …
  - places — mountain, jungle, coast …
  - hiking trails — the Route of Parks, the Pacific Crest Trail
  - a description of a place
  - the Seven Natural Wonders — Paricutín, the Grand Canyon
  - words that are nouns and verbs — impact, research …

How to edit a video

- Be clear about what you want to achieve and keep it quite simple – don't try to include too many special effects or too much material.
- As you work, put clips, sound files and images in separate folders, and label them so you can find what you need. Keep copies of each file, just in case.
- Find an editing tool online and experiment with editing. Remember, you can upload what you like and try different combinations, as you will still have the original files.
- Show your film to different people and ask for feedback. Make any final changes.

Project planner

Unit 5 Graphic organiser

Mind map centred on **What makes a good communicator?** with branches:
- a history of sharing news
- advertising as communication
- a school website
- a report
- word formation: prefixes — mistranslate, overdo …
- ways of talking — whistle out of tune, mutter under your breath …
- reporting verbs — admit, refuse …

How to use body language and gestures

- Stand or sit up straight. Walk towards your audience to make a point, but don't turn your back on them while you're talking.
- Stand in an open position with your arms in front of you. You can use your hands to explain things, but don't play with them or put them in your pockets.
- If you want to persuade someone with your presentation, you'll need to look confident. Make eye contact with your audience and smile.
- Use positive gestures like nodding and smiling to create a good atmosphere. To signal the end of your presentation, put your hands together to encourage the audience to clap.

Unit 6 Graphic organiser

Mind map centred on **What can you do to challenge yourself?** with branches:
- challenges — achieve a goal, take a risk …
- television — rehearsal, perform …
- people — acquaintance, teammate …
- do we need a rival to be successful?
- people who have done difficult challenges — Lynne Cox, Nirmal Purja

How to engage your audience

- Tell the audience what to expect and describe the different stages of the presentation clearly.
- Tell a story (*I was watching a TV show recently when …*).
- Address the audience directly (*You've probably seen talent shows, but …*).
- Interact with the audience: look round the room; ask a question (*Do you think there are too many talent shows on TV?*) and listen to people's answers; ask people to vote on something …
- Use different materials (slides, charts, a video clip, photos …) and presenters.
- When you speak, vary your tone and speed, emphasise key words and pause after important information.
- Add humour or emotion (*We're excited to tell you about this amazing new show …*).

Project planner

Unit 7 Graphic organiser

- **Could you unplug for a day, a week, a month or even longer?**
  - being off the grid
    - National Day of Unplugging
    - a holiday off the grid
  - chilling out, getting active
    - disconnect, get into …
  - lifestyle
    - stressful, conventional …
  - expressions with *make* and *do*
    - do my best, make an effort …

How to create a convincing argument
- Keep your argument simple: don't introduce too many different ideas into the same sentence.
- Use imperatives to tell your audience what to do.
- Use short sentences which contrast two ideas, e.g. *Stand up instead of sitting down*.
- Make your arguments attractive to different types of people.
- Ask questions to get your audience thinking and to keep them listening.

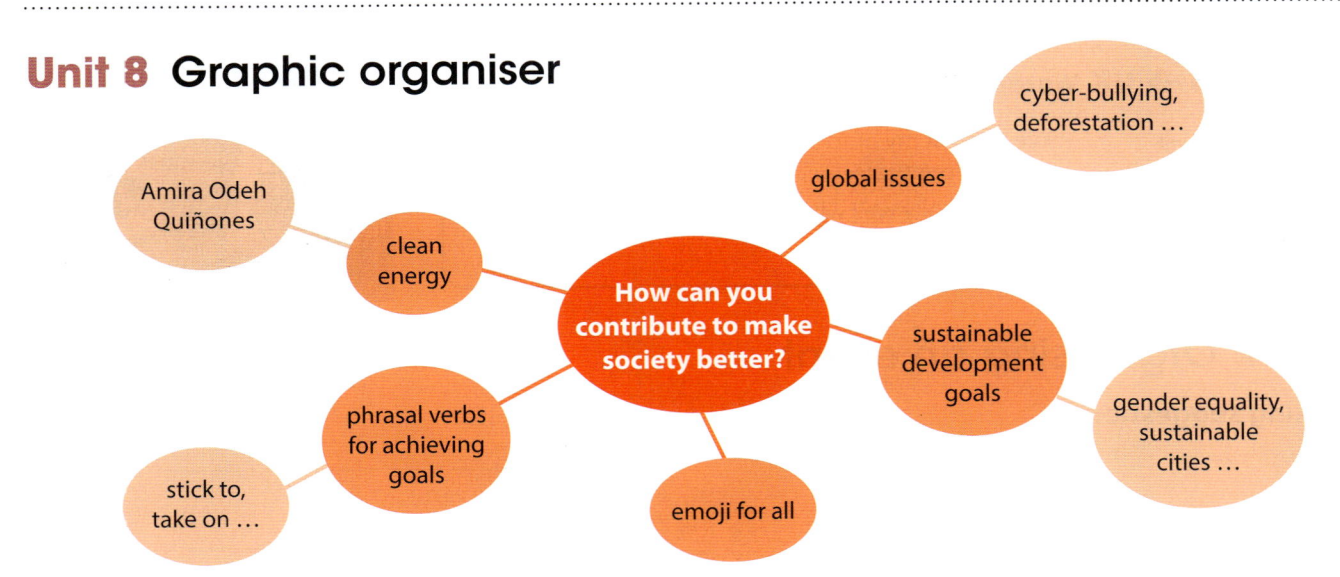

Unit 8 Graphic organiser

- **How can you contribute to make society better?**
  - global issues
    - cyber-bullying, deforestation …
  - sustainable development goals
    - gender equality, sustainable cities …
  - emoji for all
  - phrasal verbs for achieving goals
    - stick to, take on …
  - clean energy
    - Amira Odeh Quiñones

How to create a digital poster
- Choose free online software to create your digital poster.
- Identify who your target viewer is. Who is going to read the poster? What kind of content do they want/need to see?
- Think about your message: what do you want people to know after reading the poster?
- Draft an outline on paper, including the title, key information and the images you will need. What has to be on the poster?
- Choose your background image, colours, main image(s) and text fonts/sizes. Experiment until you are happy that they work well with your message.
- Decide on the layout.

Phrasebook

Unit 1 Solving shopping issues

Asking about the issue

- Can I ask why you are returning it?

- Have you got the receipt?

Issues

- I'd like to return …

- I'm afraid there's a problem with …

- (It) broke/shrank/came off …

- (It's) badly made.

- (It) doesn't fit properly.

- (It) isn't right.

- I can't give you a refund without a receipt.

- I'm afraid I've lost the receipt.

Solutions

- I can give you a refund or replace it for you.

- You can exchange it for something else.

- I can give you a credit note.

🇺🇸 ➡ 🇬🇧 **US ➡ UK Words from the unit**

| high school ➡ secondary school | I've been at my high school (US) / secondary school (UK) for four years. |
| neighbor ➡ neighbour | I get on really well with my neighbors (US) / neighbours (UK). |

Unit 2 Organising an event

Making suggestions

- Didn't we say … ?

- Shall we go for that then?

- Can't we go somewhere else?

- Can we at least … ?

- How about … ? / What about … (for a change)?

Negotiating

- Won't we be … then?

- Who's going to … ?

- Like where/what/who?

- What's wrong with … anyway?

Agreeing and disagreeing

- You're on!

- I'm not so sure about that.

- I guess you're right.

Phrasebook

🇺🇸 ➜ 🇬🇧 US ➜ UK Words from the unit

field ➜ pitch	We used to play baseball on the biggest field (US) / pitch (UK) in the city.
outlet ➜ socket	I plugged my phone into the outlet (US) / socket (UK).

Unit 3 Telling an anecdote

Describing what happened
- Guess who I've just seen!
- Before you ask, he/she/it was …
- He/She/It was a … who …
- Now he/she …
- I was out with … when …
- He/She was … (having lunch).
- I couldn't believe it!
- It was unbelievable!

Showing interest
- Who?
- Who's that?
- Yeah, but who is he/she?
- Where did you see him/her?
- Who was he/she with?
- What was he/she doing?
- Cool!/Wow!/Amazing!
- Did you get a selfie?

🇺🇸 ➜ 🇬🇧 US ➜ UK Words from the unit

soccer ➜ football	In my opinion, soccer (US) / football (UK) is much more exciting than basketball.
program ➜ programme	I really like the TV program (US) / programme (UK) that's on Saturdays at 8:00 pm.

Unit 4 Giving instructions

- Make sure you/Be sure to …
- Whatever you do, don't …
- Don't forget (to)/Remember (to) …
- Under no circumstance should you …
- It's important to …

- It helps to …
- You need to …
- Try (not) to …
- Always/Never …

🇺🇸 ➜ 🇬🇧 US ➜ UK Words from the unit

harbor ➜ harbour	I might go to see the boats in the harbor (US) / harbour (UK) later.
vacation ➜ holiday	My best vacation (US) / holiday (UK) was when I went to Florida when I was 14.

Phrasebook

Unit 5 Discussing opinions

Giving your opinion
- I suppose that's …
- The way I see it …
- I'm sure (that) …

Asking others for their opinion
- What do you think?
- How do you feel about … ?
- What would you say if … ?
- But what if … ?

Agreeing/Disagreeing
- I see what you mean.
- You have a point there.
- You know, I think you're right.
- I suppose so, but …
- True/Maybe, but …

> **US → UK Words from the unit**
>
> chips → crisps — Could you go and buy some chips (US) / crisps (UK) for the party?
>
> 10th Grade → Year 11 — Students who are 15 and 16 are normally in 10th Grade (US) / Year 11 (UK).

Unit 6 Checking understanding and clarifying

Checking understanding
- What do you mean when you say … ?
- You mean … ?
- If I understand you correctly …
- So you're saying that …
- You've lost me!
- I'm not sure what you mean.
- Can you explain again?
- Could you go over that again?

Clarifying
- What I mean is …
- What I meant was …
- Do you get what I'm saying?
- Are you following me?
- Do you see what I mean?
- Yes, that's exactly what I mean/meant.
- No, that's not quite what I meant!

> **US → UK Words from the unit**
>
> buddy → mate — I've known my best buddy (US) / mate (UK) for 11 years.
>
> practice (v.) → practise (v.) — If you want to get better at playing a musical instrument, you need to practice (US) / practise (UK).

Phrasebook

Unit 7 Giving directions

Asking for directions
- Sorry to bother you, but I'm looking for …
- Excuse me! Do you know this area?
- Can you tell me … ?
- Do you know the way to … ?

Being unable to help
- I'm afraid I can't help you.
- I'm not from around here.

Giving directions
- Go back the way you came to the …
- Turn left/right and keep walking until …
- It's on your left/right.
- Cut through …
- Walk around the …
- Go across the …
- You'll end up/come out by …
- You can't miss it!

US → UK Words from the unit

cell phone → mobile phone
jewelry → jewellery

It would be hard for me to switch off my cell phone (US) / mobile phone (UK) for a whole week.

There's a market in my city which sells some beautiful jewelry (US) / jewellery (UK).

Unit 8 Politely interrupting

Politely interrupting
- Sorry to interrupt, but …
- Do you mind if I/Could I just add/ask something?
- If I could interrupt for a moment?
- Before you go on, I'd like to say something …
- Sorry to cut you off, but …

Continuing to speak
- Sorry, but I haven't finished yet.
- Wait a minute …
- As I was saying …
- I'll just finish what I have to say …

US → UK Words from the unit

math → maths
hold on → hang on

I really enjoy studying math (US) / maths (UK).

Hold on (US) / Hang on (UK), we should read through this again to check for mistakes.

125

Irregular verbs

Infinitive	Past simple	Past participle
be /biː/	was / were /wɒz/, /wɜː(r)/	been /biːn/
beat /biːt/	beat /biːt/	beaten /ˈbiːt(ə)n/
become /bɪˈkʌm/	became /bɪˈkeɪm/	become /bɪˈkʌm/
begin /bɪˈgɪn/	began /bɪˈgæn/	begun /bɪˈgʌn/
bet /bet/	bet /bet/	bet /bet/
break /breɪk/	broke /brəʊk/	broken /ˈbrəʊk(ə)n/
bring /brɪŋ/	brought /brɔːt/	brought /brɔːt/
broadcast /ˈbrɔːdˌkɑːst/	broadcast /ˈbrɔːdˌkɑːst/	broadcast /ˈbrɔːdˌkɑːst/
build /bɪld/	built /bɪlt/	built /bɪlt/
buy /baɪ/	bought /bɔːt/	bought /bɔːt/
catch /kætʃ/	caught /kɔːt/	caught /kɔːt/
choose /tʃuːz/	chose /tʃəʊz/	chosen /ˈtʃəʊz(ə)n/
come /kʌm/	came /keɪm/	come /kʌm/
cost /kɒst/	cost /kɒst/	cost /kɒst/
cut /kʌt/	cut /kʌt/	cut /kʌt/
do /duː/	did /dɪd/	done /dʌn/
draw /drɔː/	drew /druː/	drawn /drɔːn/
drink /drɪŋk/	drank /dræŋk/	drunk /drʌŋk/
drive /draɪv/	drove /drəʊv/	driven /ˈdrɪv(ə)n/
eat /iːt/	ate /eɪt/	eaten /ˈiːt(ə)n/
fall /fɔːl/	fell /fel/	fallen /ˈfɔːl(ə)n/
feed /fiːd/	fed /fed/	fed /fed/
feel /fiːl/	felt /felt/	felt /felt/
fight /faɪt/	fought /fɔːt/	fought /fɔːt/
find /faɪnd/	found /faʊnd/	found /faʊnd/
fly /flaɪ/	flew /fluː/	flown /fləʊn/
forget /fə(r)ˈget/	forgot /fə(r)ˈgɒt/	forgotten /fə(r)ˈgɒt(ə)n/
get /get/	got /gɒt/	got /gɒt/
give /gɪv/	gave /geɪv/	given /ˈgɪv(ə)n/
go /gəʊ/	went /went/	gone /gɒn/
grow /grəʊ/	grew /gruː/	grown /grəʊn/
hang /hæŋ/	hung /hʌŋ/	hung /hʌŋ/
have /hæv/	had /hæd/	had /hæd/
hear /hɪə(r)/	heard /hɜː(r)d/	heard /hɜː(r)d/
hit /hɪt/	hit /hɪt/	hit /hɪt/
hold /həʊld/	held /held/	held /held/
hurt /hɜːt/	hurt /hɜːt/	hurt /hɜːt/

Irregular verbs

Infinitive	Past simple	Past participle
keep /kiːp/	kept /kept/	kept /kept/
know /nəʊ/	knew /njuː/	known /nəʊn/
lay /leɪ/	laid /leɪd/	laid /leɪd/
learn /lɜː(r)n/	learnt /lɜː(r)nt/	learnt /lɜː(r)nt/
leave /liːv/	left /left/	left /left/
let /let/	let /let/	let /let/
lose /luːz/	lost /lɒst/	lost /lɒst/
make /meɪk/	made /meɪd/	made /meɪd/
mean /miːn/	meant /ment/	meant /ment/
meet /miːt/	met /met/	met /met/
pay /peɪ/	paid /peɪd/	paid /peɪd/
put /pʊt/	put /pʊt/	put /pʊt/
read /riːd/	read /red/	read /red/
ride /raɪd/	rode /rəʊd/	ridden /ˈrɪd(ə)n/
ring /rɪŋ/	rang /ræŋ/	rung /rʌŋ/
run /rʌn/	ran /ræn/	run /rʌn/
say /seɪ/	said /sed/	said /sed/
see /siː/	saw /sɔː/	seen /siːn/
sell /sel/	sold /səʊld/	sold /səʊld/
send /send/	sent /sent/	sent /sent/
set /set/	set /set/	set /set/
shine /ʃaɪn/	shone /ʃɒn/	shone /ʃɒn/
show /ʃəʊ/	showed /ʃəʊd/	shown /ʃəʊn/
sing /sɪŋ/	sang /sæŋ/	sung /sʌŋ/
sit /sɪt/	sat /sæt/	sat /sæt/
sleep /sliːp/	slept /slept/	slept /slept/
speak /spiːk/	spoke /spəʊk/	spoken /ˈspəʊk(ə)n/
spend /spend/	spent /spent/	spent /spent/
stand /stænd/	stood /stʊd/	stood /stʊd/
steal /stiːl/	stole /stəʊl/	stolen /ˈstəʊl(ə)n/
stick /stɪk/	stuck /stʌk/	stuck /stʌk/
sweep /swiːp/	swept /swept/	swept /swept/
swim /swɪm/	swam /swæm/	swum /swʌm/
take /teɪk/	took /tʊk/	taken /ˈteɪk(ə)n/
teach /tiːtʃ/	taught /tɔːt/	taught /tɔːt/
tell /tel/	told /təʊld/	told /təʊld/
think /θɪŋk/	thought /θɔːt/	thought /θɔːt/
throw /θrəʊ/	threw /θruː/	thrown /θrəʊn/
understand /ˌʌndə(r)ˈstænd/	understood /ˌʌndə(r)ˈstʊd/	understood /ˌʌndə(r)ˈstʊd/
wake /weɪk/	woke /wəʊk/	woken /ˈwəʊk(ə)n/
wear /weə/	wore /wɔː/	worn /wɔːn/
win /wɪn/	won /wʌn/	won /wʌn/
write /raɪt/	wrote /rəʊt/	written /ˈrɪt(ə)n/

Macmillan Education Limited
4 Crinan Street
London N1 9XW

Companies and representatives throughout the world

Get Involved! Student's Book B2 ISBN 978-1-380-06523-0
Get Involved! Student's Book B2 with Student's App and Digital Student's Book
ISBN 978-1-380-06895-8

Text © Emma Heyderman, Gill Holley, Kate Pickering, Patricia Reilly 2021
Design and illustration © Macmillan Education Limited 2021

The authors have asserted their right to be identified as the authors of this work in accordance with the Copyright, Designs and Patents Act 1988.

First published 2021

All rights reserved. No part of this publication may be reproduced, stored in a retrieval system, or transmitted in any form or by any means, electronic, mechanical, photocopying, recording, or otherwise, without the prior written permission of the publishers.

Original design by Designers Collective Ltd and emc design ltd
Page make-up by emc design ltd
Illustrated by Esther Cuadrado (Beehive Illustration) pp65, 122; Carl Pearce (Beehive Illustration) p12; Szilvia Szakall (Beehive Illustraion) p117–118; Laszlo Veres (Beehive Illustration) p23
Cover design by Designers Educational
Cover photographs by Getty Images/Halfpoint Images (tr), Getty Images/Maskot (bl), Getty Images/Westend61 (m); Shutterstock.com/Dean Drobot (tl), Shutterstock.com/Rawpixel.com (br).
Picture research by Penelope Bowden, Proudfoot Pictures

Authors' acknowledgements
Emma Heyderman would like to thank her family for their continued support.
Patricia Reilly would like to thank all of the team at Macmillan Education for their hard work and dedication to the project. She would also like to thank her family, especially Alisha, who makes everything worthwhile (and makes a great cup of tea!).

The authors and publishers would like to thank the following for permission to reproduce their photographs:
Airwair International Limited p112(c); **From the Alamy Stock Photo collection:** Andrew Unangst pp39(t), 2(tl), Christian Kober p63(background), Edward Herdwick p63(bl), Ian Dagnall Commercial Collection pp11(7), 89, INNA FINKOVA p35(girl), Inge Johnsson pp58, 59, Ivan Chiosea p35(boy), Michael Routh p49(fire), Tony French pp11(5), 63(tr), trekkerimages p49(landslide), Stephan Karg p35(bl), Stocktrek Images, Inc. p108(6), Tetiana Chemerys p35(stopwatch); **DLA** pp49(br), 73(br), 85(br), 97(br); **Ella London** pp11(1), 15(t), 115(tc); **Getty Images**/ABDESIGN p107(r), adamkaz p13(r), ALEAIMAGE p80(inset), Alys Tomlinson p75(tr), amnachphoto p32, Andrew Brookes p24(b), Andriy Onufriyenko p25(d), AndreyTTL p83(lc), Artis777 p36(tc), asbe pp15(rm), 31(tr), BackyardProduction p25(d), beastfromeast pp106, 107(background), Beeldbewerking p103(tr), Big Five Images p79(tm), bjones27 p112(d), Carlo A p16, Carol Yepes p80(t), coryz p112(b), d3sign p2(br), daboost p114(l), damircudic p73(bl), Damocean p112(b), David Malan p44(t), DGLimages p41(brm), DoraDalton p54(d), dottedhippo pp24(a), 25, dramalens p36(c), EDUARDO MUNOZ ALVAREZ/Stringer p99(blm), Eloi Omella p57, Erik Isakson p91(tr), FatCamera pp41(tm), 108(3), filo pp82, 83(background), fmajor p52, Geber86 p10, gemenacom pp94, 95(background), George Mdivanian/EyeEm p95(inset), GlowingEarth pp2(bl), 59(tr), Guerilla p108(4), Hill Street Studios p73(tlc), Izabelite pp27(b), 115(br), Jasmin Merdan p7(boy), Jasmina007 p36(tr), Jeff Penner/EyeEm p59(l), Jena Ardell p61(c), Joe Daniel Price p107(l), Jose A. Bernat Bacete pp34, 35 (background), Joshua Sammer/Contributor pp11(6), 77(tl, bl), 115(br), Justin Lewis p72(tr), kali9 p97(b), KatarzynaBialasiewicz p9, Kriangkrai Thitimakorn p78(b), Leung King Lun p51(a), Lysogor pp48, 49(avalanche), Marc_Hilton pp11(4), 51(g), Maskot pp7(girl), 108(5), martin_adams2000 pp3(bm), 88, mikkelwilliam p92, MiguelABriones p56(ti), Mint Images pp60(a), 61, Mmdi p27(t), Mohd Hafiez Mohd Razali/EyeEm p109(bl), monkeybusinessimages pp41(br), 108(1), moodboard p44(inset), monsitj p25(c), NachoUli p109(br), naruecha jenthaisong p71(mr), Noppasin Wongchum p114(lc), Paul Souders pp 2(mr), 109(lm), Pawel Gaul pp51(d), 115(inset, background), piola666 p71(tr, blc), Piotrurakau pp12, 13 (background), Poike p55(tr), RapidEye p61(d), Rayman p75(b), RilindH p71(tl), RoschetzkyIstockPhoto pp96, 97(background), R.M. Nunes p51(f), runeer p60(c), ryasick p108(2), Salvatore Virzi/EyeEm p48(volcano), Sam Edwards p43(tr), Sawitree Pamee/EyeEm p75(tl), Scott Legato/Contributor pp11(3), 39(bl), SDubi pp48, 49(quake), sergeyryzhov p19(r), shironosov p83(mr), smartboy10 pp22, 23(background), SolStock pp6(ml), 36(br), Stephen Frink p56(inset), Stephen Zeigler P37(tl), sturti p104, Sumetee Theesungnern/EyeEm p80(br), Suttipong Sutiratanachai pp46, 47(background), T2 Images p68, Tetra Images p111, The Washington Post/Contributor pp11(8), 101, Thomas Barwick p108(7), Ulrike Schmitt-Hartmann p87, Tonda p51(c), track5 p17, Vchal p53, Viaframe pp48, 49(falls), Vincent Pommeyrol pp48, 49(reef), VvoeVale p79(tr), WALTER ZERLA p95, Westend61 pp20, 108(8), wundervisuals p83(tl), Xsandra p73(tl), 450yamaha pp72, 73(lc), Yaorusheng p48(river), Zzvet p51(e); **Macmillan Education Limited** pp3(tr, mr, ml), 12(b, bm), 19(l), 22, 24(tl, lm, bl), 31(tl), 34(ml), 36(bl, lm), 37(r), 43(tl), 46(l), 47(b, t), 48(ml, b), 55(tl), 58(ml), 60(lm, bl), 61(r), 67(tl), 70, 71(boy, girl), 72(ml, bl), 79(tl), 82(l), 84(lm, bl), 91(tl), 94, 96(bl, ml), 103(tl), 106, 113(a, b, c, d, e, f); Courtesy of **Maitane Alonso Monasterio** pp39(rm), 115(bl); Courtesy of **No Isolation**/Estera Kluczenko pp11(2), 29(tr); **Shutterstock.com**/Alex_Traksel p28, Cosmic_Design p99, Elise Amendola/AP p29(tmr), Goran Bogicevic p85(tl), HIGOOD studio p32, HQuality p27(r), Jacob Lund p85(lm), Mauricio Graiki p85(bl), modustollens p15(bl), Ollyy p61(bl), Pierre Leclerc p59(rm), PKpix p84(rc), Polly Thomas p6(bm), Rawpixel.com p99(t), Richard Whitcombe p97(a), Rubi Rodriguez Martinez p51(b), Samuel Borges Photography p99; **STOCKBYTE** p67(tr); Courtesy of **UNITED NATIONS DEPARTMENT OF GLOBAL COMMUNICATIONS** p96(c); Courtesy of **WASP** p109(rm).

Video footage and stills supplied by:
Digeo Productions pp13, 25, 37, 61; **DLA** pp49, 73, 85, 97; **MTJ** pp19, 31, 43, 55, 67, 79, 91, 103; **Maia Films** pp22, 34, 46, 47 (tr, br), 58, 70, 71(girl, boy) 82, 94, 106.

BBC of the British Broadcasting Corporation, The Olympic Games of The International Olympic Committee, Instagram of Facebook Inc., FIFA World Cup of FIFA, Formula 1 of Formula One World Championship Limited, YouTube of Google LLC TikTok of TikTok, Hulu of Hulu, LLC, Facebook of Facebook Inc., Apple of Apple Inc., iPad of Apple Inc., adidas of the adidas Group, PUMA of PUMA Europe GmBH, Dr. Martens of Airwair International Ltd, Whatsapp of Facebook Inc. are trademarks which do not sponsor, authorise or endorse this publication.

Additional sources:
p15 – Haller, K. (2018). meet ella london, the yellow lady, karenhaller.co.uk, Card, G. (2019). Experience: I wear purple every day, The Guardian, theguardian.com.
p18 – Statistics from Pothitos, A. (2016). The History of the: Smartwatch, mobileindustryreview.com; Thompson, J. (2018). Watches A Concise History of the Smartwatch, bloomberg.com; Connor, A. (2018). The History of the Smartwatch Goes Back Much Further Than You'd Think, www.gearpatrol.com.
p27 –Statistics from Roser, M. (2019). Future Population Growth, ourworldindata.org.
p40 –Statistics from Smith, K. (2019). 53 Incredible Facebook Statistics and Facts, brandwatch.com; Sweney, M. (2018). Is Facebook for old people? Over-55s flock in as the young leave, theguardian.com; mediakix.com website, What is the best social media channel for influencer marketing?; Kolowich Cox, L. (2019). The Best Time to Post on Instagram, Facebook, Twitter, LinkedIn, & Pinterest, blog.hubspot.com.
pp41, 42 –Statistics from Boztas, S. (2018). Why Dutch teenagers are among the happiest in the world, theguardian.com; McKenna, J. (2018), This is why Dutch teenagers are among the happiest in the world, weforum.org; Westscott, K. (2007). Why are Dutch children so happy?, news.bbc.co.uk; Schacter,H. L. (2018). Teens who feel down may benefit from picking others up, theconversation.com.
p42 – Statistics from 13 Celebrities You Didn't Know Were Best Friends Seventeen, seventeen.com.
p75 – Statistics from Hunt, E. (2019). Great rivals: how a nemesis can make you more effective and successful, theguardian.com; Carnevale, J. B. (2019). Competitive Rivals Can Make You More Successful, entrepreneur.com.
p87 – Statistics from withoutmedia.wordpress.com website, 4. Advantages of unplugging.
p99 – Statistics from Agnew, P. (2018). 6 Facts About Emojis Found Using New Analysis, brandwatch.com; blog.adobe.com website, (2016). Infographic: 92% Of World's Online Population Use Emojis; vivaldi.com website, (2018). Emoji – the global pop stars of digital communication; Pardes, A. (2018). The WIRED Guide to Emoji, wired.com; Buchholz, K. (2020). In 2021, Global Emoji Count Will Grow to 3,353, statista.com; Burge, J. (2019). 230 New Emojis in Final List for 2019, blog.emojipedia.org; Webb, K. (2019). Here's every single new emoji we're getting this year, businessinsider.com; Busby M. (2019). Campaign group in Finland crowdsource for 'forgiveness' emoji, theguardian.com.
p109 – Statistics from Emmons, R. (2010). Why Gratitude Is Good, greatergood.berkeley.edu.
p112– Statistics from Newman, C. (2019). One million seeds to be planted in UK's biggest seagrass restoration scheme, swansea.ac.uk; Falkenberk, K. (2013). How To Get Your Teen To Unplug (And Like It), forbes.com; Cochrane, L. (2020). Carpe DM: 60 years of the Dr Martens boot – fashion's subversive smash hit, theguardian.com; bbc.com website, (2020). Tree planting: 'I want to plant one million', (2020). Seagrass: A million seeds planted off Pembrokeshire coast; indiewire.com website, (2013). Gender Inequality in Film: In Infographic Form; Whiting, K. (2019). 7 surprising and outrageous stats about gender inequality, weforum.org; Dr. Smith, S. L., Choueiti, M., Dr. Pieper, K. Gender bias without borders, seejane.org; womenandhollywood.com website, Women Onscreen.

These materials may contain links for third party websites. We have no control over, and are not responsible for, the contents of such third party websites. Please use care when accessing them.

The inclusion of any specific companies, commercial products, trade names or otherwise does not constitute or imply its endorsement or recommendation by Macmillan Education Limited.

Printed and bound in Spain

2025 2024 2023 2022 2021
10 9 8 7 6 5 4 3 2 1